What do you know about Ethical Frames in AI?

Overview of machine learning

Machine Learning is a branch of Artificial Intelligence (AI) that focuses on the development of computer systems capable of learning from data and making predictions or taking actions without being explicitly programmed. In this tutorial, we will provide an overview of machine learning and its key concepts, techniques, and applications.

1. Understanding Machine Learning:

- Definition of Machine Learning: Explain what machine learning is and how it differs from traditional programming.

- Importance of Machine Learning: Discuss the significance of machine learning in various domains, such as healthcare, finance, and self-driving cars.

2. Types of Machine Learning:

- Supervised Learning: Describe supervised learning, where the algorithm learns from labeled examples to make predictions or classifications.

- Unsupervised Learning: Introduce unsupervised learning, where the algorithm discovers patterns or relationships in unlabeled data.

- **Reinforcement Learning:** Explain reinforcement learning, where the algorithm learns by interacting with an environment to maximize rewards.

3. Key Concepts in Machine Learning:

- **Features and Labels:** Define features and labels, which are the input and output variables used by the machine learning algorithm.

- **Training Data:** Discuss the importance of training data and how a model learns from it.

- **Model Evaluation:** Explain how to evaluate the performance of a machine learning model using metrics like accuracy, precision, and recall.

4. Machine Learning Algorithms:

- **Regression Algorithms:** Discuss linear regression, polynomial regression, and logistic regression algorithms for continuous and categorical output predictions.

- **Classification Algorithms:** Introduce popular classification algorithms such as decision trees, random forests, support vector machines, and naive Bayes.

- **Clustering Algorithms:** Explain clustering algorithms like k-means, hierarchical clustering, and DBSCAN that group similar data points together.

5. Machine Learning Process:

- Data Preprocessing: Describe the steps involved in preparing and cleaning the data before training a model, including handling missing values and feature scaling.

- Model Training: Explain how to train a machine learning model using various algorithms and techniques.

- Model Evaluation and Improvement: Discuss the methods for evaluating model performance, tuning hyperparameters, and preventing overfitting.

6. Applications of Machine Learning:

- Image and Video Recognition: Highlight the use of machine learning in computer vision tasks like object detection, facial recognition, and image classification.

- Natural Language Processing: Explain how machine learning enables language translation, sentiment analysis, and chatbots.

- Recommendation Systems: Discuss how machine learning is used in recommendation systems to suggest personalized products, movies, or music to users.

7. Challenges and Ethical Considerations in Machine Learning:

- Bias in Data: Discuss the potential biases in training data and their impact on machine learning models and decision-making.

- Privacy and Security: Address the concerns regarding data privacy and security as machine learning algorithms require access to large amounts of data.

- Transparency and Explainability: Emphasize the importance of interpretable machine learning models and the ability to explain their decisions.

In conclusion, machine learning is a powerful technology that plays a crucial role in the field of AI. This tutorial provided an in-depth overview of machine learning, covering key concepts, algorithms, the machine learning process, applications, and ethical considerations. By understanding the fundamentals of machine learning, you can unlock its potential to solve complex problems and make data-driven decisions.

Importance of ethical considerations in machine learning

The Importance of Ethical Considerations in Machine Learning

As we delve into the world of artificial intelligence (AI) and machine learning (ML), we must also consider the crucial aspect of ethics. Ethical considerations play a significant role in ensuring the responsible and fair implementation of machine learning algorithms and systems. In this tutorial, we will explore why ethical considerations are of utmost importance in the field of machine learning, with a focus on its connection to AI.

1. Bias and Discrimination:

One fundamental reason why ethical considerations are critical in machine learning is the potential for bias and discrimination. Machine learning models are trained using data, and if that data contains biases, the models can learn and perpetuate those biases. For instance, if a hiring model is trained on data that reflects historical gender or racial biases, it can perpetuate discriminatory practices. By incorporating ethical considerations, we can reduce such biases and ensure fairness in ML applications.

2. Privacy and Data Protection:

A significant concern in the era of AI and ML is the protection of personal data and privacy. Machine learning algorithms often require vast amounts of data, including personal information. It is crucial to have ethical guidelines in place to ensure that data is handled securely and confidentially. This includes obtaining informed consent, anonymizing data, and implementing strong security measures to safeguard sensitive information.

3. Accountability and Transparency:

Another vital aspect of ethical considerations in machine learning is accountability and transparency. ML models tend to be complex and operate in a black-box manner, making it challenging to understand how they reach their conclusions. This lack of transparency can lead to distrust and raise questions about ethical implications. By striving for transparency, we can ensure that ML models are accountable for their decisions and provide explanations for their output.

4. Fairness and Equality:

Machine learning algorithms can have far-reaching impacts on individuals and society. Ethical considerations emphasize the importance of fairness and equality in the deployment of ML models. It is essential to address potential biases and ensure that the benefits and opportunities provided by ML are distributed equitably. By prioritizing fairness, we can avoid reinforcing existing inequalities and work towards creating a more just society.

5. Human Control and Responsibility:

Despite the impressive capabilities of ML models, ethical considerations remind us of the importance of human control and responsibility. Machines should augment human decision-making rather than replace it entirely. Human oversight is necessary to ensure that machine learning systems align with ethical principles and do not act in ways that are harmful, unethical, or violate human rights.

Conclusion:

In conclusion, ethical considerations play a vital role in the field of machine learning and its connection to AI. By emphasizing fairness, transparency, privacy, accountability, and human control, we can ensure that ML algorithms are developed and deployed in an ethical manner. By incorporating ethical considerations into AI and ML practices, we can create systems that benefit individuals and society as a whole, while minimizing potential harms and inequities. It is imperative to prioritize ethics in machine learning to foster responsible and sustainable AI development.

Ethical Frameworks in Machine Learning

Understanding Ethical Frameworks in Machine Learning

Ethical frameworks provide a structured approach for analyzing ethical dilemmas and making ethical decisions. In the context of machine learning, ethical frameworks help guide the development, deployment, and use of machine learning algorithms and systems responsibly and fairly. This tutorial will explore various ethical frameworks specifically relevant to machine learning.

1. Rawlsian Justice: Rawlsian justice, inspired by the work of philosopher John Rawls, focuses on ensuring fairness and equality in societal arrangements. In machine learning, this framework emphasizes the need to minimize biases and discrimination that can arise from biased training data or algorithmic decision-making. Developers and practitioners of machine learning systems must strive to ensure equal treatment and opportunities for all individuals, irrespective of their demographic or socioeconomic backgrounds.

2. Privacy and Consent: Privacy and consent are crucial considerations in machine learning. This framework emphasizes the importance of obtaining explicit and informed consent from individuals whose data is being used for training or inference purposes. It also highlights the need to maintain the privacy and confidentiality of personal data, ensuring it is used only for intended purposes and with appropriate safeguards against misuse or unauthorized access.

Lack of privacy risks misuse of personal data.

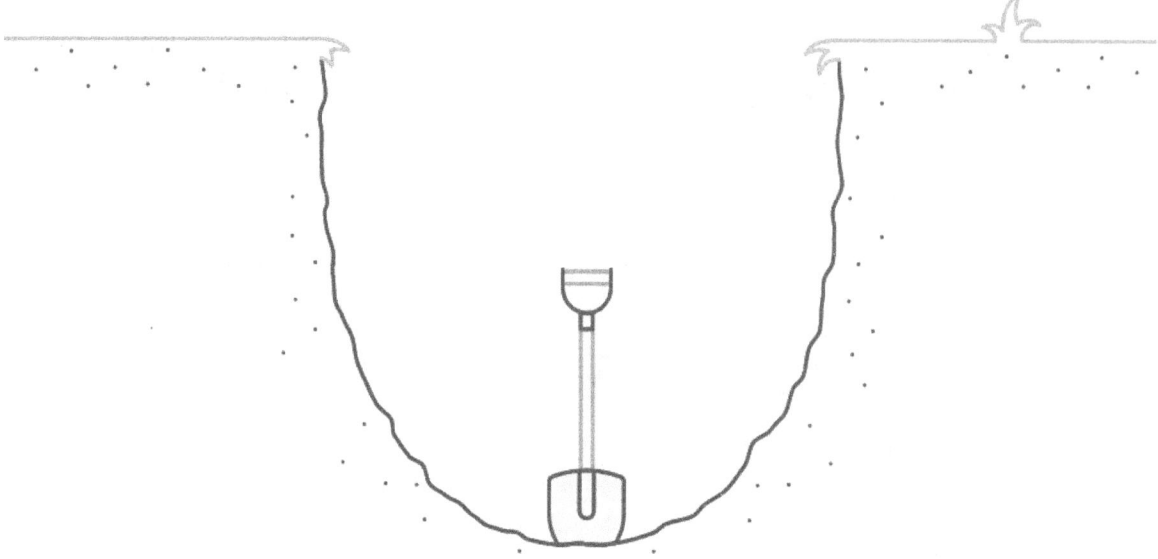

3. Accountability and Transparency: This framework focuses on the importance of accountability and transparency in machine learning systems. Developers should ensure that the decision-making process of algorithms is explainable and interpretable. This includes providing clear explanations for the reasons behind algorithmic decisions and enabling individuals to challenge or appeal decisions when necessary. Furthermore, developers should be accountable for any harm caused by their algorithms and should strive to rectify any biases or unintended consequences that may arise.

Accountability and Transparency in ML

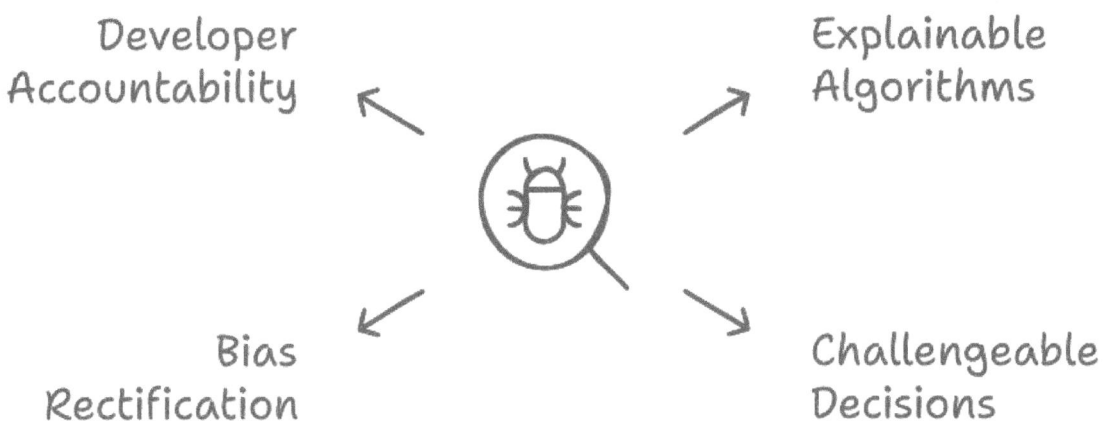

4. Fairness and Bias: Fairness and bias are critical considerations in machine learning systems. This framework emphasizes the need to mitigate biases that can be present in training data or inadvertently introduced by the algorithms themselves. Developers should proactively identify and rectify biases, ensuring that decisions made by machine learning systems do not disproportionately favor or discriminate against certain individuals or groups.

Addressing Fairness and Bias in ML

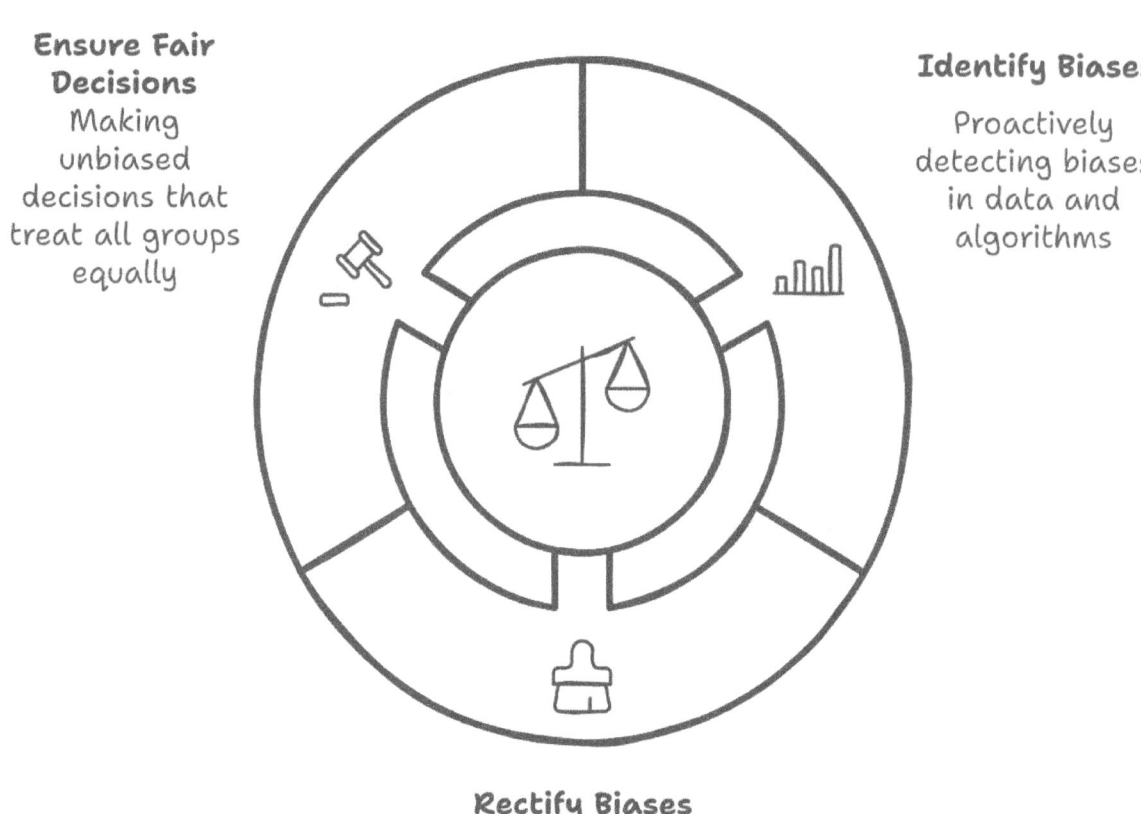

5. Human Values and Ethical Considerations: This framework emphasizes the importance of aligning machine learning systems with human values and ethical considerations. Machine learning algorithms should be designed to respect cultural norms, legal requirements, and ethical guidelines. They should prioritize the welfare and well-being of individuals, promote social good, and avoid harm or negative impacts on society.

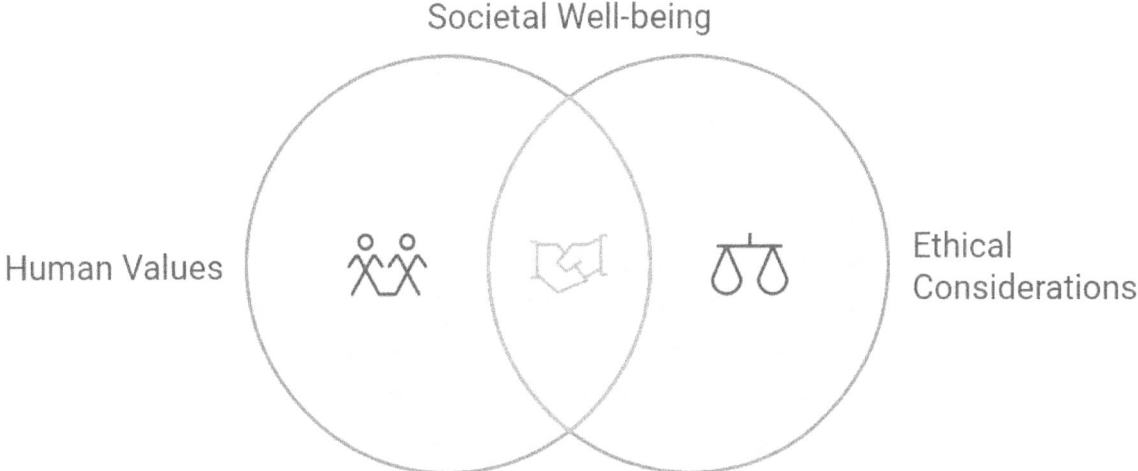

By applying these ethical frameworks in the development and use of machine learning systems, we can ensure responsible, fair, and ethical deployment of these technologies. Developers, researchers, policymakers, and other stakeholders need to prioritize ethical considerations and continuously evaluate the impact of machine learning on individuals and society as a whole.

Please note that this tutorial is not an exhaustive exploration of all ethical frameworks. It serves as an introduction to some key frameworks specifically relevant to machine learning. Understanding and applying ethical frameworks is an ongoing and evolving process, influenced by various cultural, societal, and technological factors.

Utilitarianism

Utilitarianism is an ethical framework that focuses on maximizing overall happiness or well-being for the greatest number of people. In the context of machine learning, utilitarianism can aid in making ethical decisions when developing and implementing algorithms and systems.

Understanding the Basics of Utilitarianism: Utilitarianism is rooted in consequentialism, which means that the morality of an action is determined by its consequences. The key principle of utilitarianism is to maximize happiness and minimize suffering. It is often associated with the famous phrase, "the greatest good for the greatest number." Key Concepts in Utilitarianism:

1. Hedonistic Utilitarianism: This branch of utilitarianism emphasizes the maximization of pleasure and the minimization of pain as the ultimate measures of utility or happiness. It

takes into account the intensity, duration, and extent of happiness or suffering caused by an action or decision.

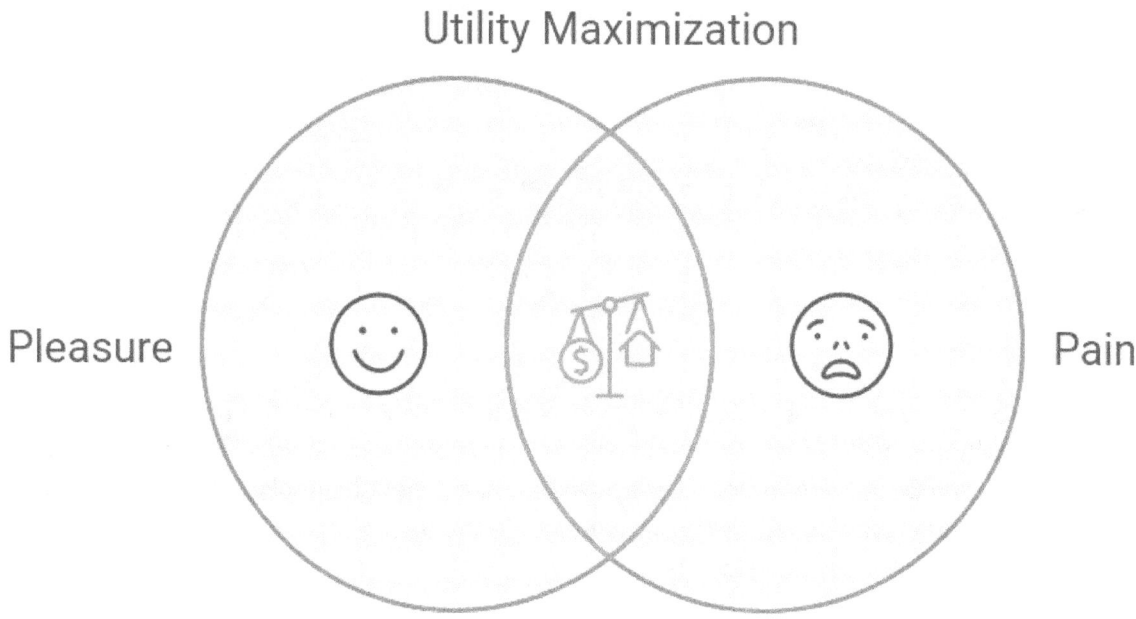

2. Act Utilitarianism: Act utilitarianism applies the principle of maximizing overall happiness to individual actions. It suggests that each action should be evaluated based on its potential consequences and the resulting happiness it generates. Consequently, the right action is the one that maximizes overall happiness.

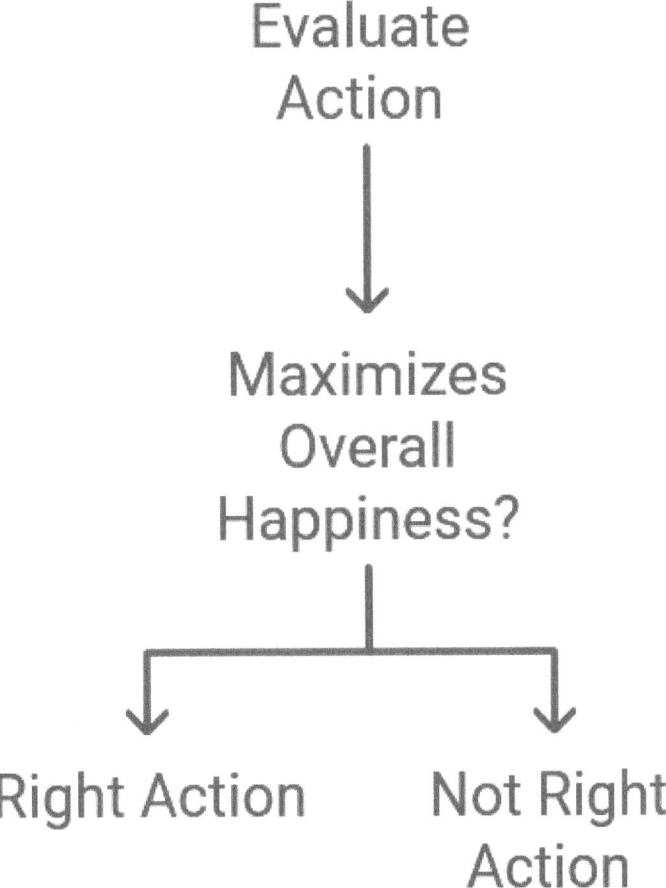

3. Rule Utilitarianism: Rule utilitarianism, on the other hand, focuses on the consequences of adopting a certain rule or principle rather than assessing individual actions. It suggests that ethical rules should be followed if they generally maximize overall happiness. In other words, actions should align with rules that promote the greatest good for society as a whole.

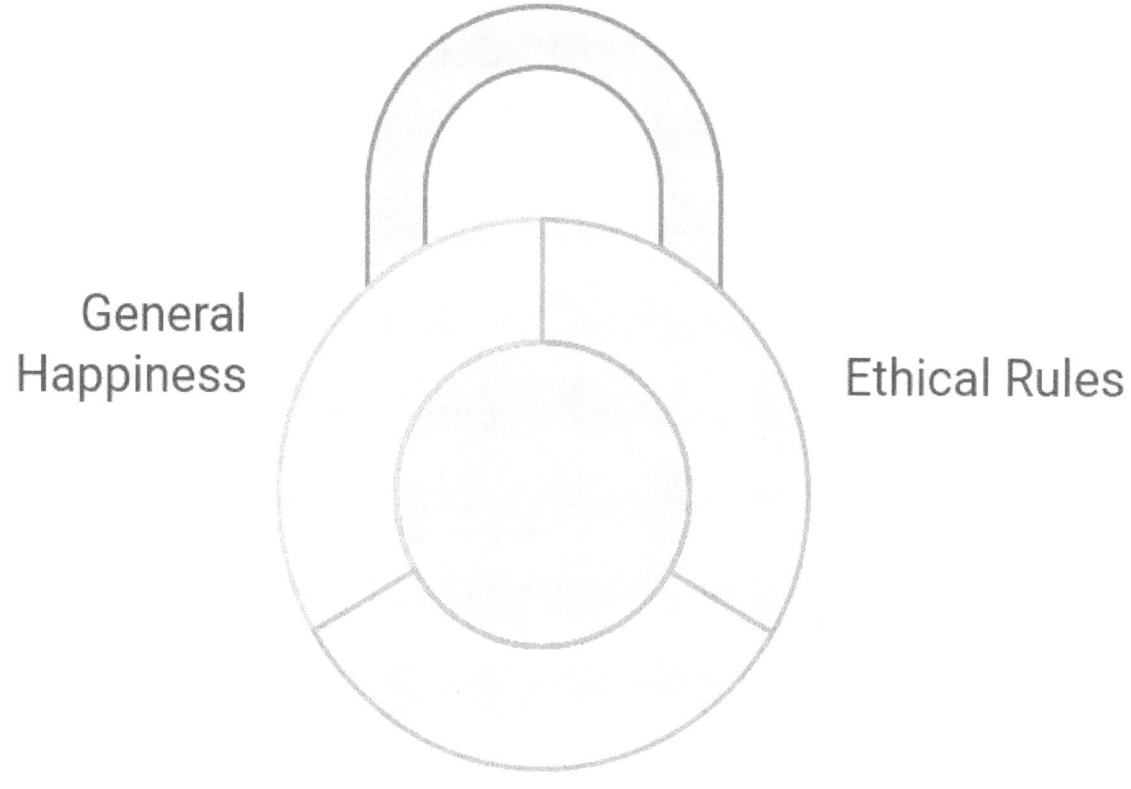

Applying Utilitarianism in Machine Learning:

1. Ethical Decision-making: Utilitarianism helps machine learning practitioners make ethical decisions by considering the potential consequences of their algorithms and systems. It encourages developers to prioritize the well-being and happiness of the users impacted by their technology.

2. Bias and Fairness: Utilitarianism can assist in mitigating algorithmic bias by making fairness a priority. By considering the overall impact on a diverse group of individuals, utilitarianism promotes an equitable distribution of benefits and reduces discrimination.

3. Privacy and Data Usage: Utilitarianism also guides the responsible use of data in machine learning. It encourages practitioners to balance the desire for data-driven insights with the potential negative consequences of privacy invasion or data misuse. Striking the right balance ensures that the use of data promotes overall happiness and does not cause harm.

4. Transparency and Accountability: Utilitarianism supports increased transparency and accountability in machine learning processes. By sharing information about algorithms, decision-making criteria, and potential consequences, developers can solicit feedback and make necessary adjustments to improve overall happiness.

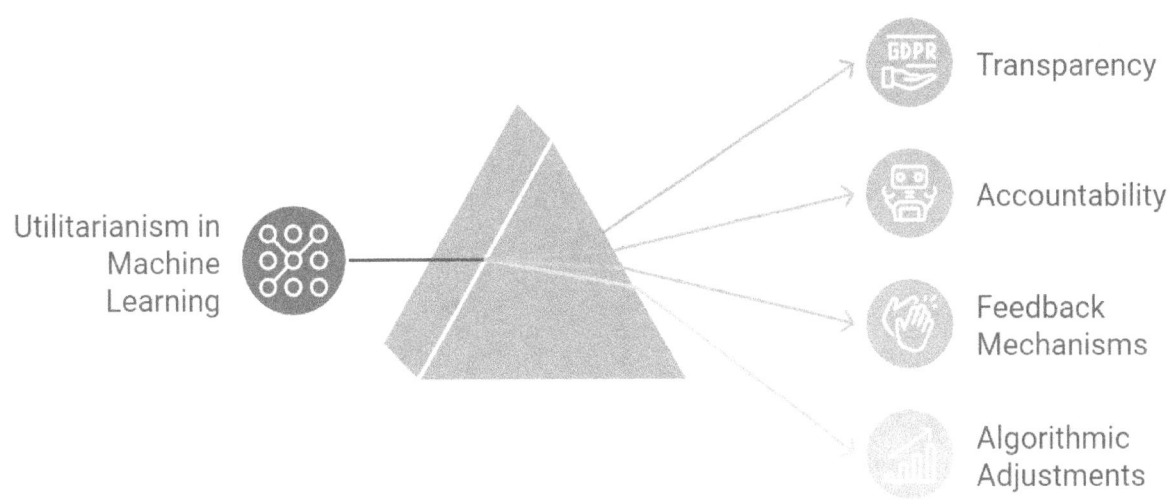

Unpacking Utilitarianism in Machine Learning

Benefits and Criticisms of Utilitarianism: Utilitarianism offers several advantages in the context of machine learning. It provides a practical framework for decision-making that focuses on maximizing overall happiness. It emphasizes the importance of considering the well-being of a diverse user base and promoting fairness and equity. Additionally, utilitarianism encourages responsible data usage and transparency.

However, utilitarianism has also faced criticism. One common critique is that it may sacrifice the rights and interests of minority groups in favor of the majority's happiness. This concern underscores the need for ethical guidelines that carefully balance utilitarianism with other ethical frameworks to ensure a fair and just outcome.

In conclusion, utilitarianism offers a relevant and practical ethical framework for making decisions in the field of machine learning. By prioritizing overall happiness and considering the consequences of actions, utilitarianism can help developers create and implement algorithms and systems that benefit society at large while minimizing harm.

Question 1

What does Rawlsian justice focus on in the context of machine learning?

Answer:

1 - The importance of obtaining explicit consent

2 - The need to prioritize human values

3 - The need to minimize biases and discrimination

The answer is number 3

Question 2

Which ethical framework emphasizes the importance of privacy and consent in machine learning?

1- Rawlsian Justice

2 - Privacy and Consent

3 - Accountability and Transparency

4 - Fairness and Bias

The correct answer is number 2

Question 3

What is the key principle of utilitarianism?

1 - Maximize overall happiness

2 - Minimize suffering

3 - Maximize overall happiness and minimize suffering

4 - Maximize pleasure

The correct answer is number 3

Ethical Frameworks in Machine Learning

Deontological ethics

Deontological ethics is an important ethical framework to consider when discussing ethical frameworks in machine learning. Unlike utilitarianism or virtue ethics, which focus on the consequences of actions or the character of the moral agent, deontological ethics centers around the duty or moral obligation of individuals and the inherent rights and wrongs of specific actions.

Deontological ethics is particularly relevant in the context of machine learning as it involves making decisions about the ethical implications of creating and deploying autonomous systems. In this tutorial, we will explore the key concepts of deontological ethics and how they apply to machine learning.

1. Deontology - Understanding the Basics: - Concept of deontology and its origins. - Key proponents of deontological ethics. - The foundational principles of deontological ethics. - Differentiating deontological ethics from other ethical frameworks.

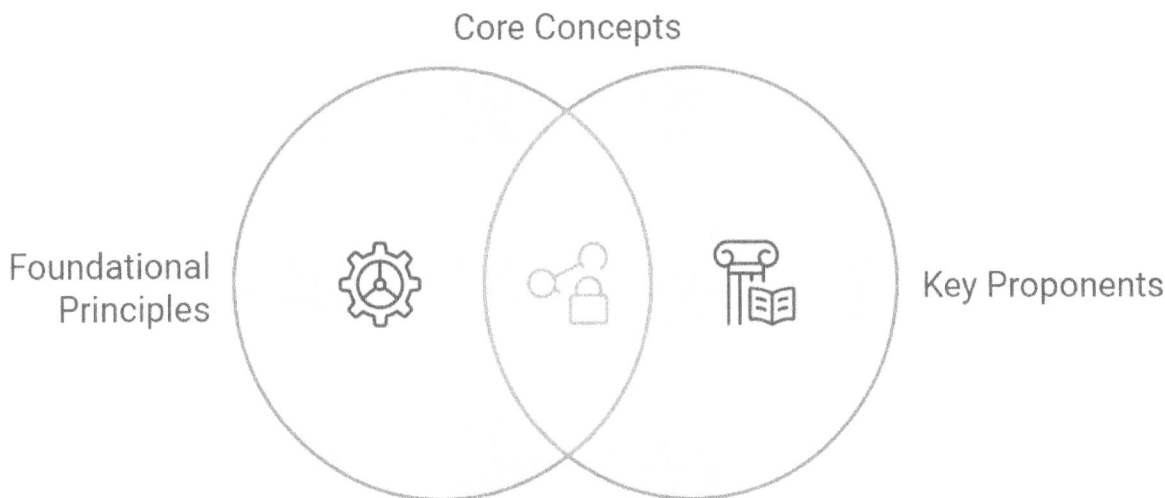

2. The Categorical Imperative: - Introduction to Immanuel Kant's categorical imperative. - Explanation of the first formulation - Act only according to that maxim by which you can at the same time will that it should become a universal law. - Explanation of the second formulation - Treat humanity, whether in your own person or in that of another, always as an end and never as a means only.

Kant's Categorical Imperative

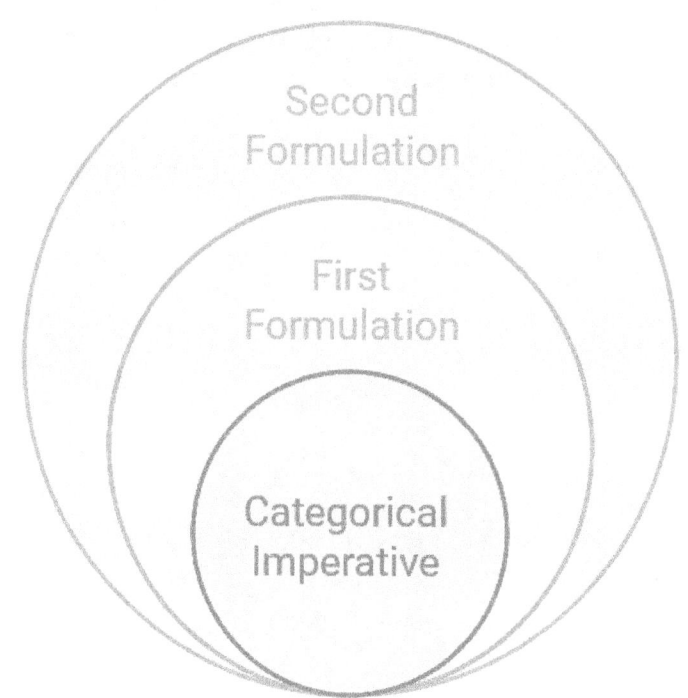

Treat humanity as an end, not a means

Act as if your action could be a universal law

Universal moral law guiding actions

3. Rights and Duties: - Understanding the concept of rights and its relation to deontological ethics. - Exploring different types of rights: natural rights, legal rights, and moral rights. - The distinction between positive and negative rights. - Duties and their connection to rights in deontological ethics.

Understanding Rights and Duties in Deontological Ethics

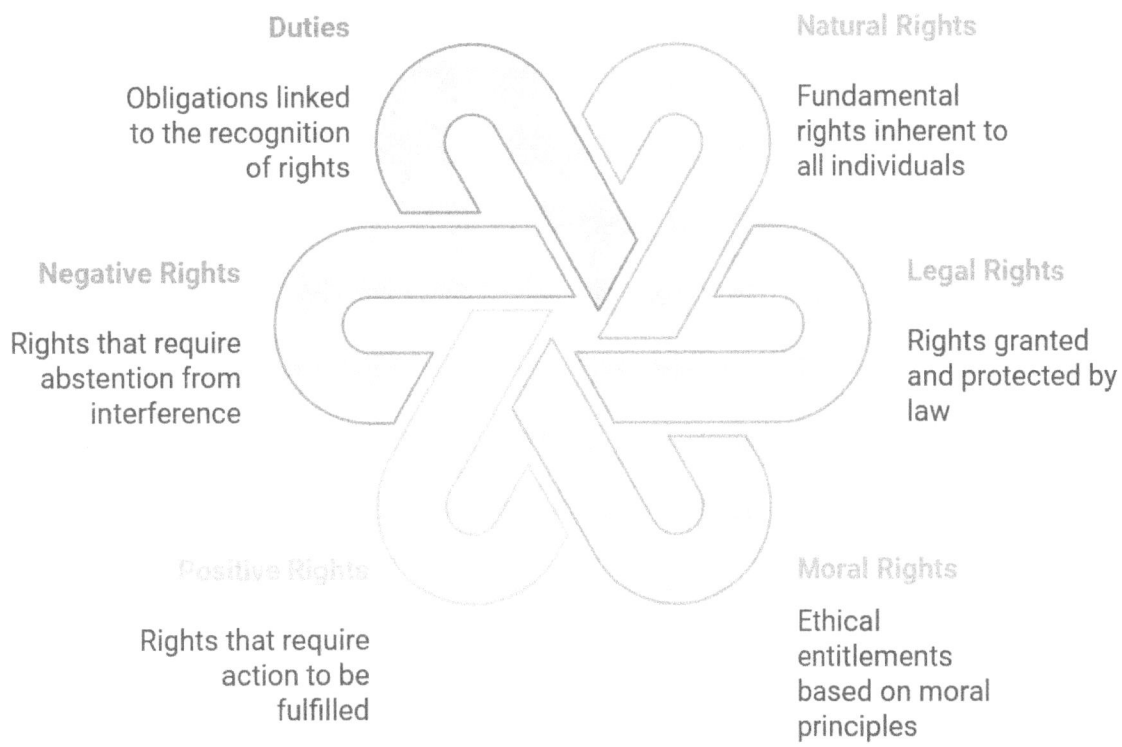

Duties — Obligations linked to the recognition of rights

Natural Rights — Fundamental rights inherent to all individuals

Negative Rights — Rights that require abstention from interference

Legal Rights — Rights granted and protected by law

Positive Rights — Rights that require action to be fulfilled

Moral Rights — Ethical entitlements based on moral principles

4. Autonomy and Moral Agency: - The importance of individual autonomy in deontological ethics. - The role of moral agency in making ethical decisions. - Examining the ethical challenges posed by autonomous systems in machine learning.

Autonomy and Moral Agency

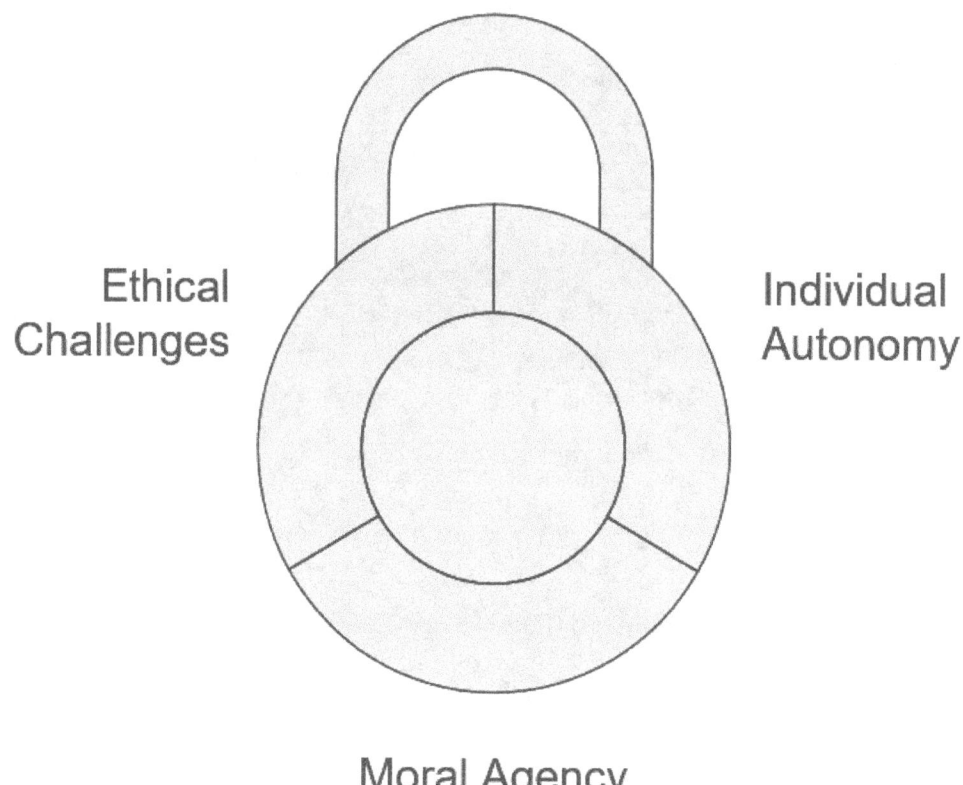

Ethical Challenges

Individual Autonomy

Moral Agency

5. The Doctrine of Double Effect: - Introduction to the doctrine of double effect. - The conditions required for the doctrine to apply. - Examining the ethical implications of applying the doctrine in machine learning scenarios.

Doctrine of Double Effect in ML

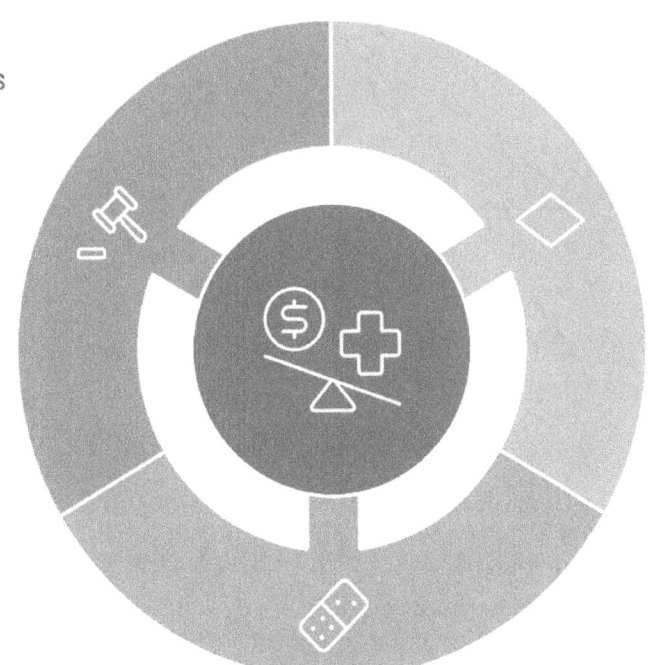

Moral Justification — Justifying actions based on ethical principles in ML

Ethical Decision-Making — Applying the doctrine to ensure ethical choices in ML systems

Unintended Consequences — Managing and mitigating unintended harm in ML applications

6. Applications of Deontological Ethics in Machine Learning: - Examining the impact of deontological ethics on the development and deployment of machine learning models. - Ethical considerations when designing and training machine learning models. - The importance of transparency and explainability in machine learning.

Deontological Ethics in Machine Learning

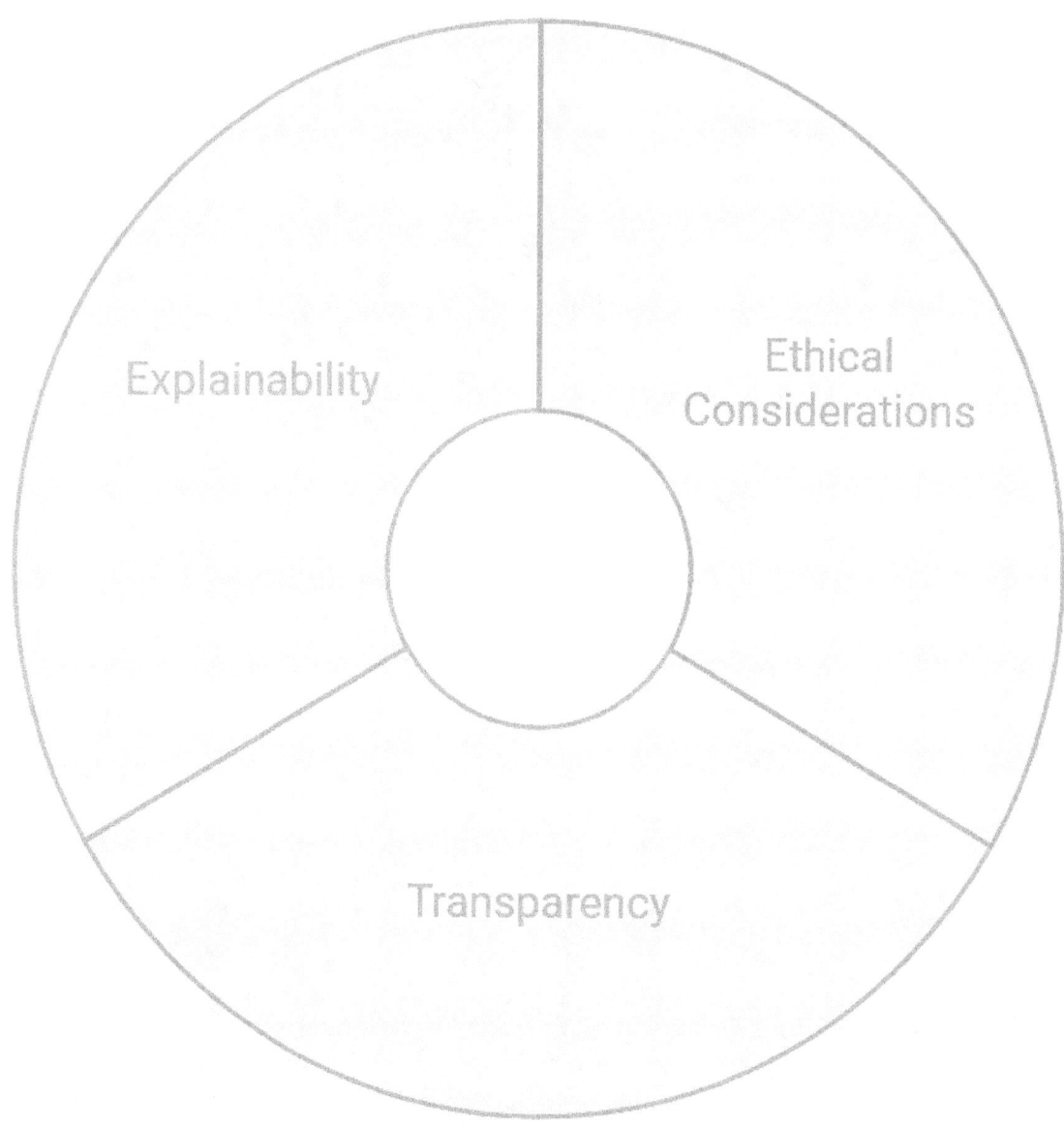

7. Case Studies: - Analyzing real-world case studies where deontological ethics have been applied to machine learning projects. - Discussing the outcomes and ethical implications of these case studies.

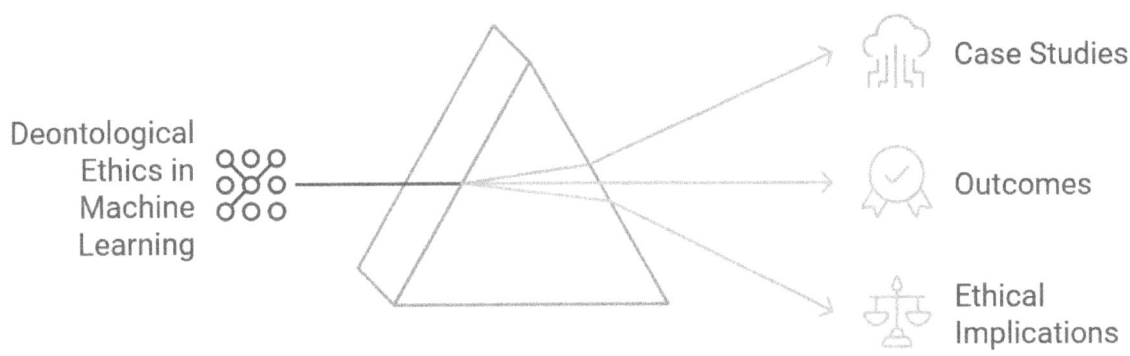

8. Criticisms and Limitations: - Exploring the criticisms of deontological ethics. - Discussing the limitations of applying deontological ethics in the field of machine learning.

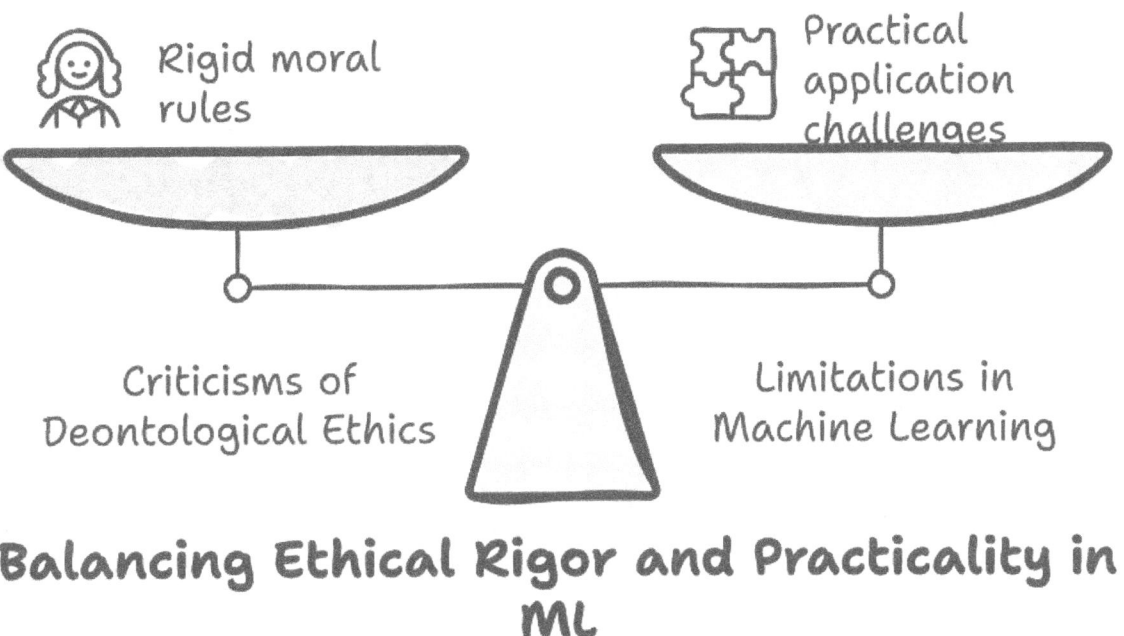

In conclusion, deontological ethics offers a valuable framework for ethical decision-making in the context of machine learning. Understanding its principles and applications can help researchers, developers, and policymakers navigate the complex ethical landscape of autonomous systems. By considering the moral obligations and inherent rights and wrongs involved, we can strive to create and deploy machine learning models that align with deontological ethical principles.

Virtue ethics

Virtue Ethics in the Context of Ethical Frameworks in Machine Learning:

When exploring ethical frameworks in the context of machine learning, one cannot overlook the importance of virtue ethics. Unlike utilitarianism and deontological ethics, which focus on the consequences of actions and adherence to rules, virtue ethics emphasizes the character of the individual making the ethical decision. This tutorial will delve into the concept of virtue ethics, its relevance to ethical frameworks in machine learning, and how it can guide ethical decision-making in this field.

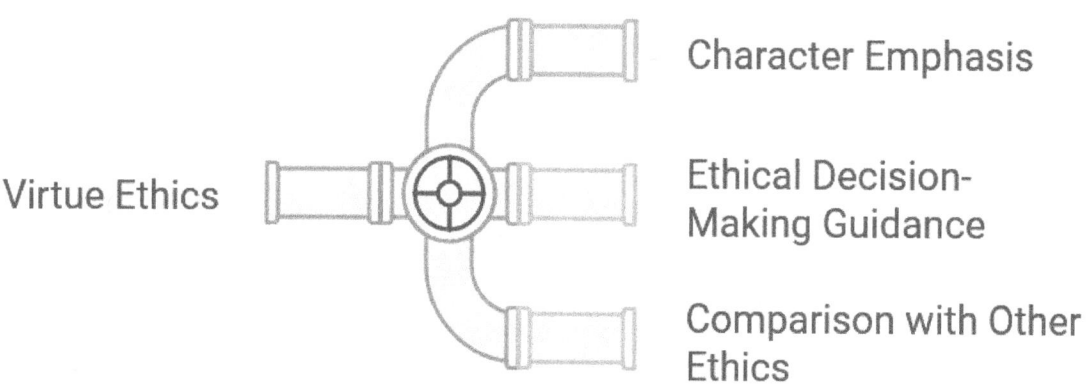

Defining Virtue Ethics:

Virtue ethics is an ethical framework that originated from ancient Greek philosophy and emphasizes the development of virtuous character traits. Such character traits include honesty, empathy, fairness, integrity, and courage. According to virtue ethics, individuals should strive to cultivate these virtues to lead ethical lives and make morally sound decisions.

Applying Virtue Ethics to Ethical Frameworks in Machine Learning: In the context of machine learning, virtue ethics suggests that ethical decision-making should be guided by the virtues that are relevant to this field. This means that individuals involved in machine learning, including researchers, engineers, and designers, should aim to develop and exhibit traits such as:

1. Objectivity: Striving for impartiality and avoiding biased decisions.

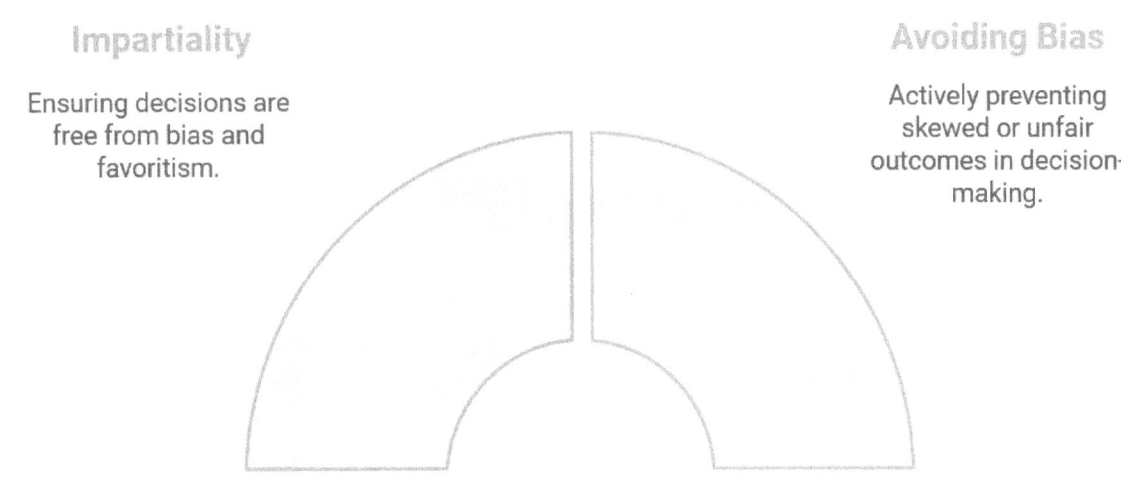

2. Transparency: Ensuring that processes, algorithms, and data used in machine learning are transparent and accessible.

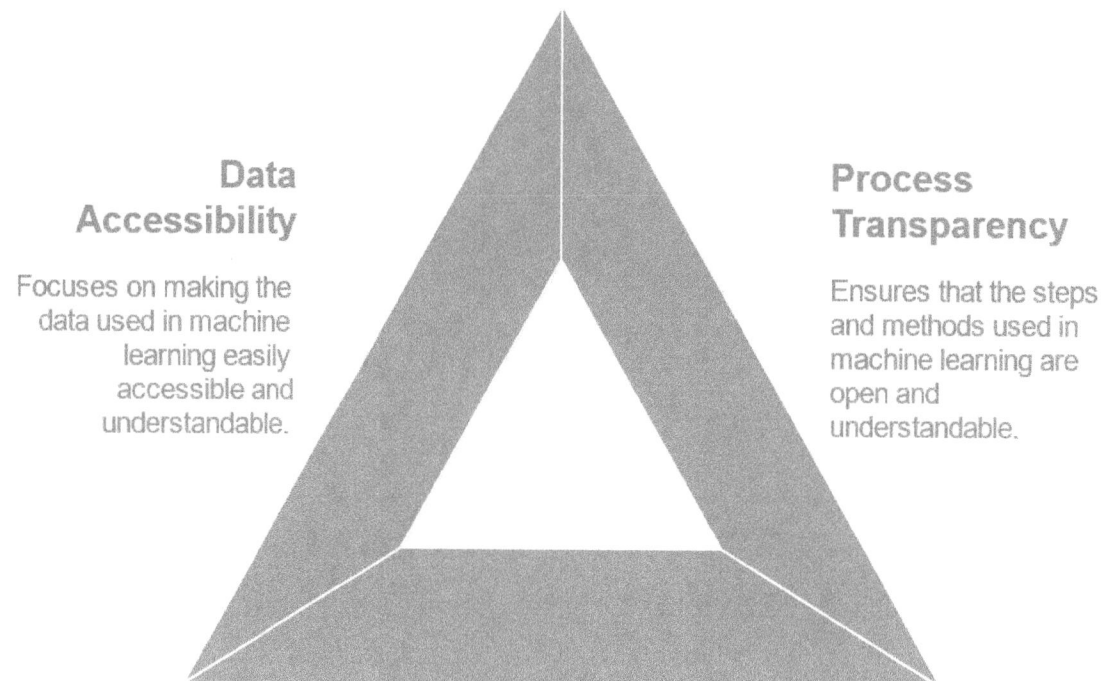

3. Accountability: Taking responsibility for the ethical implications of machine learning systems and their impact on society.

Exploring Dimensions of Accountability in ML

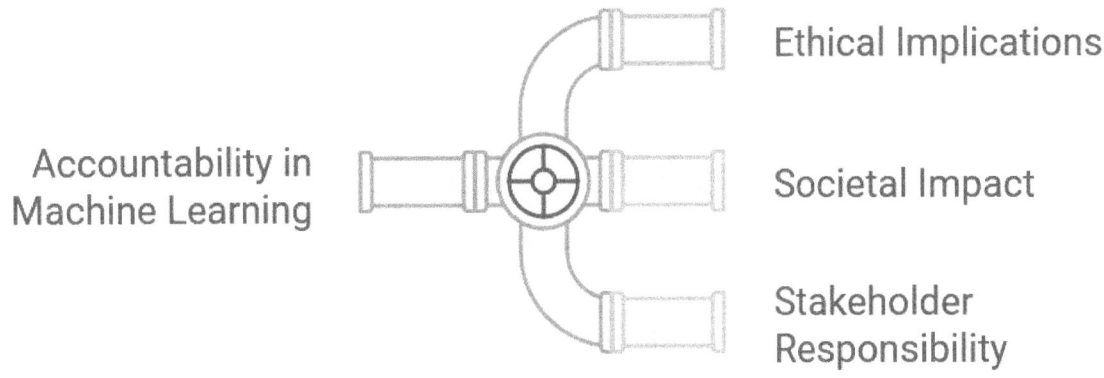

4. Fairness: Ensuring fairness in the design and implementation of machine learning models, considering factors such as bias, discrimination, and social justice.

Fairness in Machine Learning

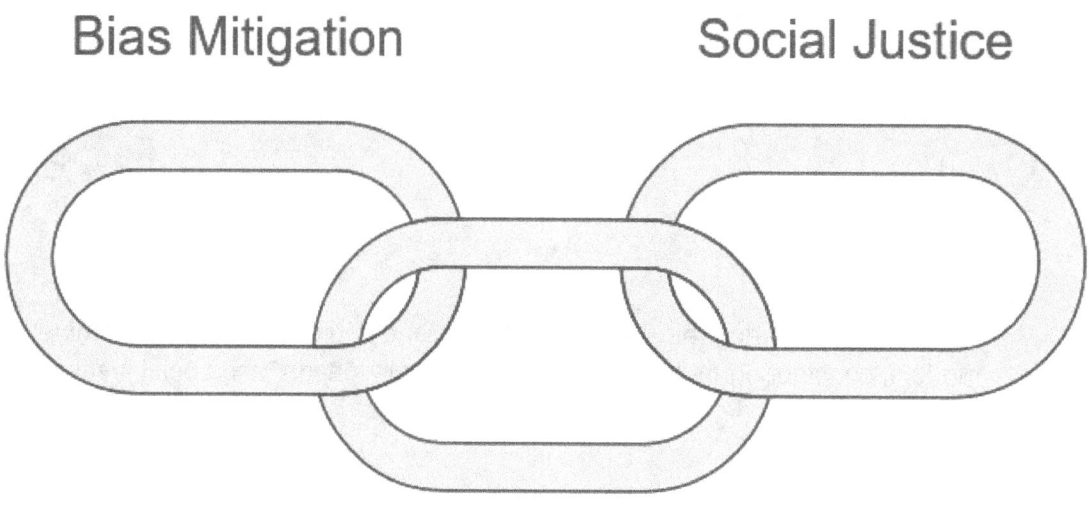

5. Privacy: Respecting and protecting individuals' privacy and personal data throughout the machine learning process.

6. Empathy: Understanding the potential impact of machine learning on individuals and society, and taking steps to mitigate harm.

7. Intellectual honesty: Upholding intellectual integrity by avoiding plagiarism, misrepresentation, or unethical practices in their research or work.

Components of Intellectual Honesty in ML

Ethical Research Practices
Conducting research with integrity

Plagiarism Avoidance
Ensuring original work is credited

Misrepresentation Prevention
Accurate and truthful representation of work

Benefits of Virtue Ethics in Machine Learning:

Incorporating virtue ethics into ethical frameworks for machine learning can have several benefits. It promotes a holistic approach to decision-making, considering not only the consequences but also the character and intentions of the individuals involved. By prioritizing virtues, machine learning professionals can aim to create systems that are not only technically advanced but also ethically responsible.

Virtue Ethics in ML Decision-Making

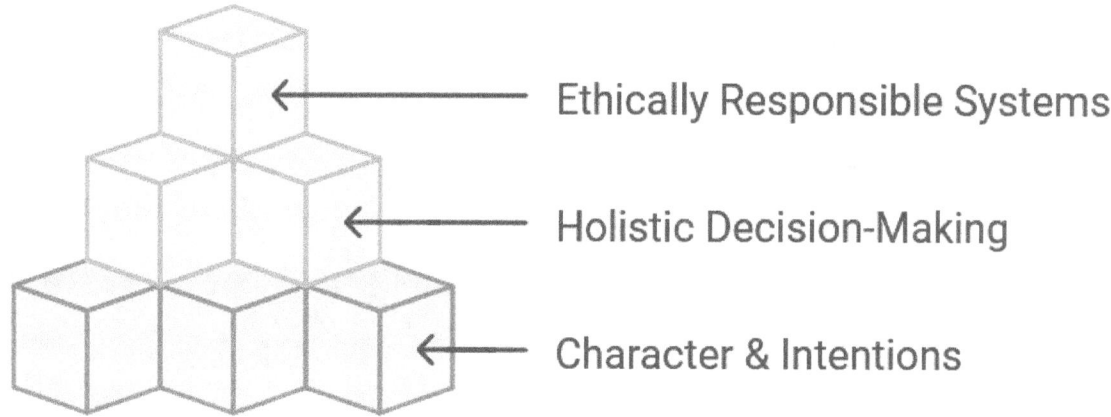

- Ethically Responsible Systems
- Holistic Decision-Making
- Character & Intentions

Guiding Ethical Decision-Making with Virtue Ethics: To make ethical decisions using virtue ethics in machine learning, individuals should ask themselves the following questions:

1. What virtues are relevant to this situation? Identify the virtues that can guide decision-making in the context of the specific ethical dilemma.

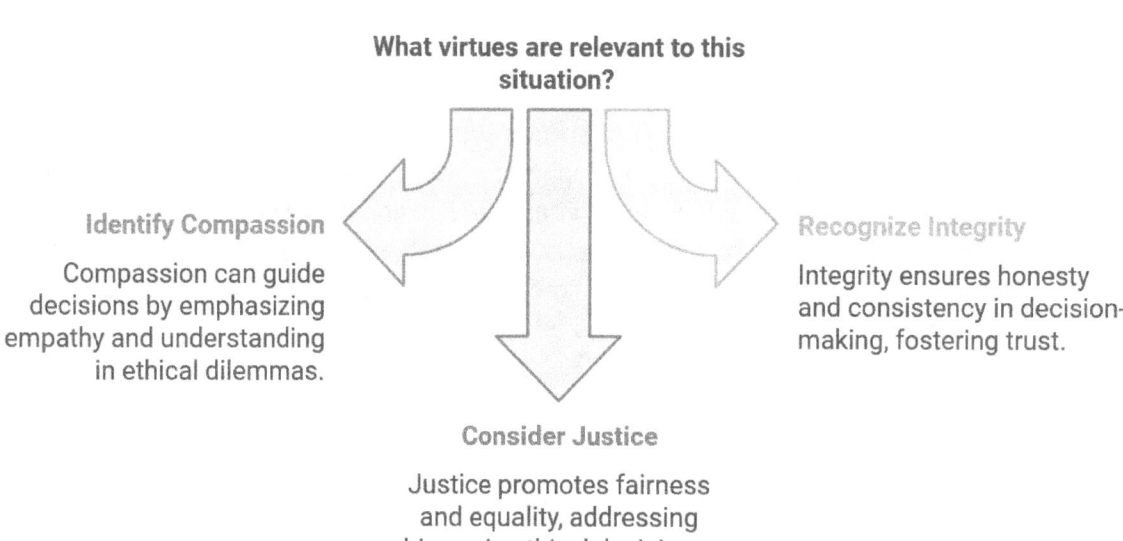

What virtues are relevant to this situation?

Identify Compassion

Compassion can guide decisions by emphasizing empathy and understanding in ethical dilemmas.

Recognize Integrity

Integrity ensures honesty and consistency in decision-making, fostering trust.

Consider Justice

Justice promotes fairness and equality, addressing biases in ethical decisions.

2. How can these virtues be cultivated and practiced? Consider ways in which the identified virtues can be developed and demonstrated in the ethical decision-making process.

3. Are there any conflicts between virtues? Reflect on potential conflicts between different virtues and strive to find a balanced approach that aligns with ethical principles.

How to resolve conflicts between virtues in ethical decision-making?

Virtue A — Promotes fairness and justice

Virtue B — Encourages innovation and progress

4. What impact will the decision have on individuals and society? Consider the potential consequences and implications of the decision on various stakeholders.

5. How can the decision be aligned with the identified virtues? Ensure that the decision aligns with the virtues that have been identified as relevant to the situation.

Virtue Alignment in Decision-Making

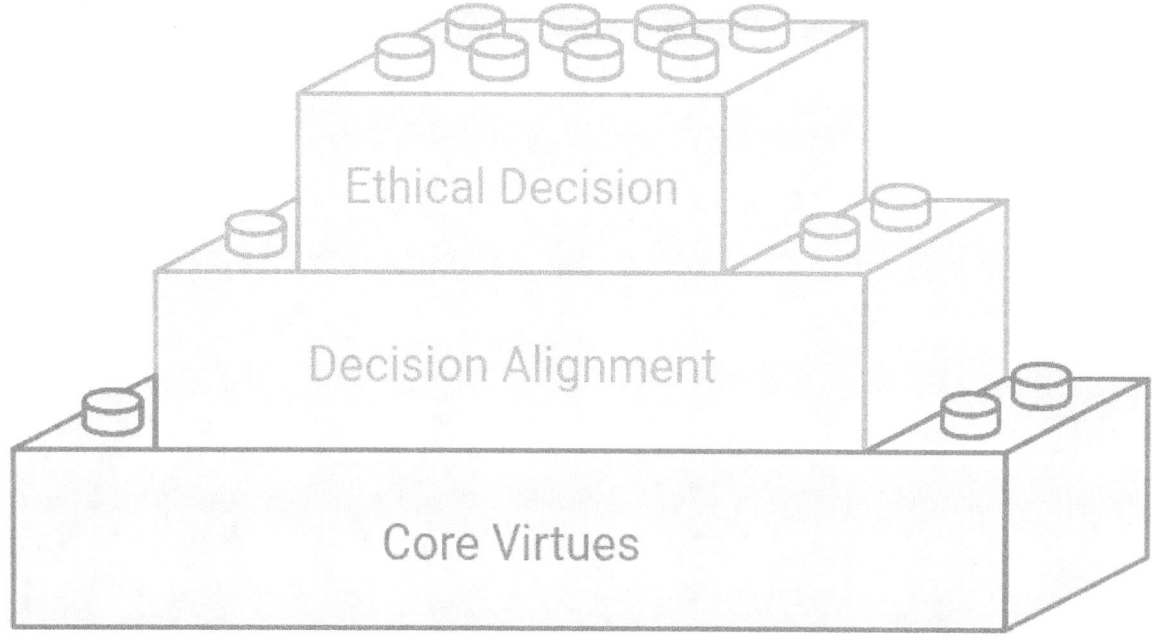

Conclusion:

Virtue ethics offers a unique perspective within the realm of ethical frameworks in machine learning. By emphasizing the development and application of virtuous character traits, it complements utilitarianism and deontological ethics, contributing to a well-rounded approach to ethical decision-making. By incorporating virtues such as objectivity, transparency, and fairness, individuals in the field of machine learning can strive to design and implement systems that are ethically responsible and considerate of societal impact.

Application of frameworks to machine learning

Consider these requirements when writing a tutorial on the topic "Application of frameworks in machine learning" with a focus on ethical perspectives:

Title: Understanding the Ethical Application of Frameworks in Machine Learning

Section 1: Applying Ethical Frameworks to Machine Learning In machine learning, ethical considerations play a significant role in ensuring that AI systems are designed and deployed responsibly. This tutorial will explore how ethical frameworks can be applied to machine learning to guide decision-making and address potential concerns. By incorporating these frameworks, we can create AI systems that are fair, transparent, and accountable.

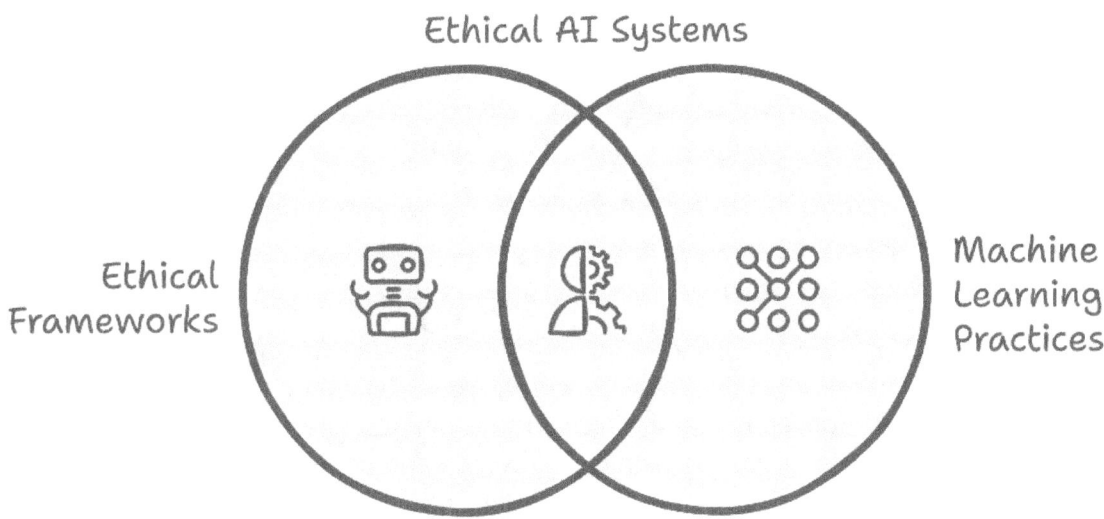

Section 2: The Importance of Ethical Frameworks in Machine Learning Machine learning algorithms have the potential to shape the decisions that impact individuals and society. As such, it is crucial to approach AI development through an ethical lens. Ethical frameworks provide a structure for evaluating the impact of machine learning algorithms on various stakeholders, mitigating potential biases, and promoting fairness and inclusivity.

Lack of ethical frameworks causes biases and unfairness.

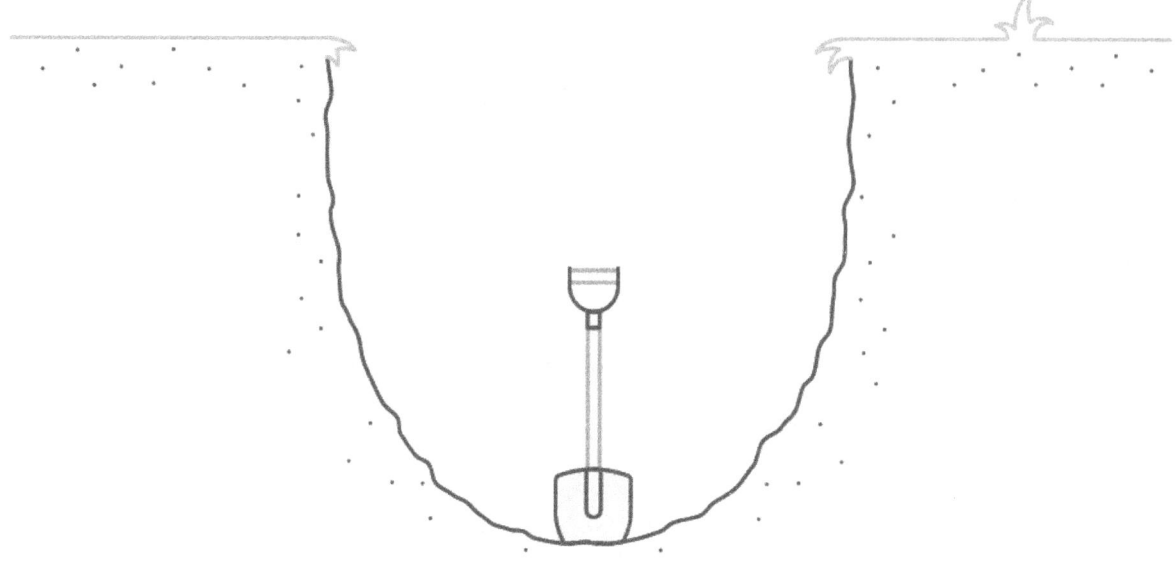

Section 3: Consequentialist Ethical Frameworks Consequentialist ethical frameworks, such as utilitarianism, focus on the outcomes and consequences of actions. In machine learning, utilitarianism can guide the optimization of algorithms based on maximizing overall social welfare. This section will explore how utilitarian principles can be applied to machine learning to balance competing interests and optimize algorithmic decision-making.

Exploring Consequentialist Ethics in Machine Learning

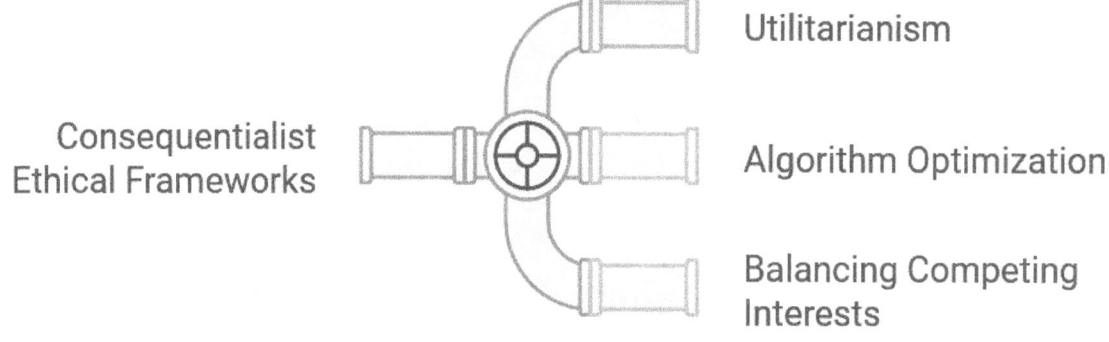

Section 4: Non-Consequentialist Ethical Frameworks Non-consequentialist ethical frameworks, including deontological ethics, emphasize adherence to principles and duties regardless of the outcomes. In machine learning, deontological ethics can guide the development of algorithms based on fundamental rights and respect for individuals. This section will explore how deontological principles can shape the decision-making process in machine learning, particularly regarding privacy, consent, and fairness.

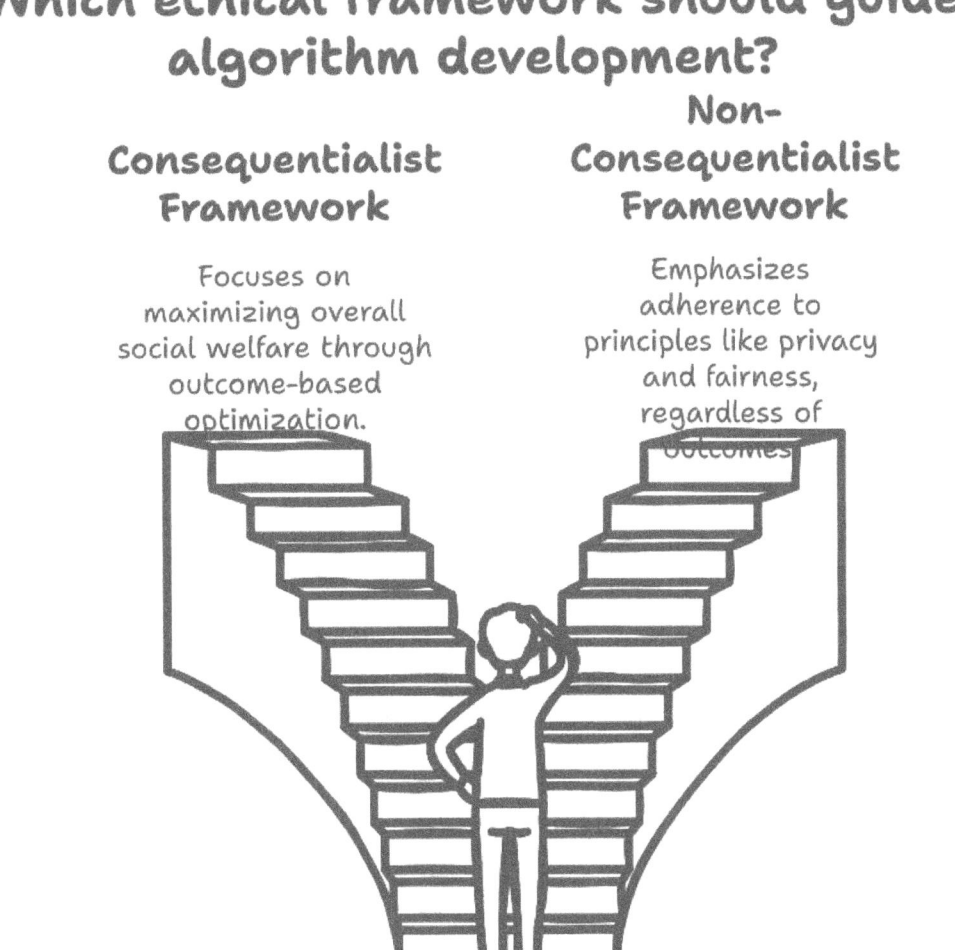

Section 5: Virtue Ethics and AI Development Virtue ethics focuses on the character and moral values of individuals involved in decision-making. In machine learning, virtue ethics can guide the development of AI systems that reflect desirable human traits, such as honesty, empathy, and accountability. This section will explore how virtue ethics can shape the training process, data collection, and deployment of machine learning models.

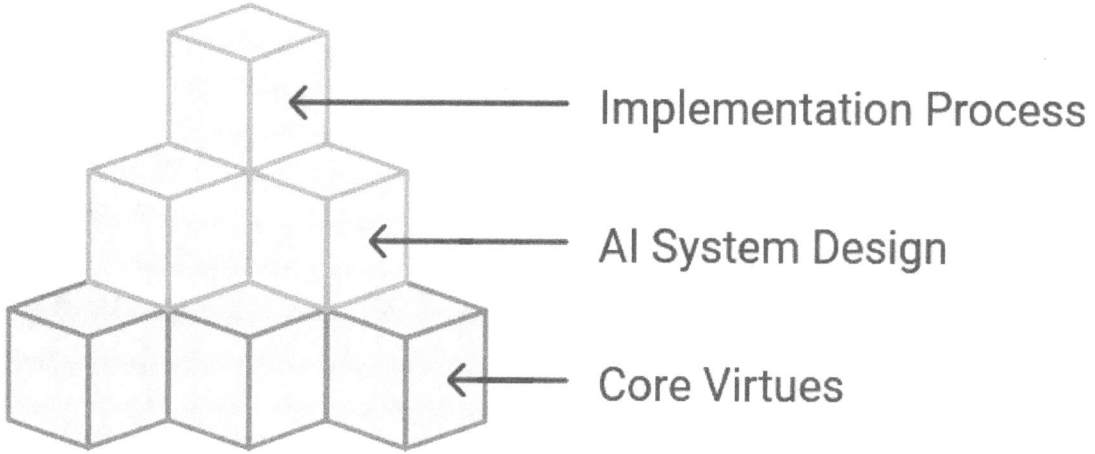

Section 6: Integrating Ethical Standards into Machine Learning Systems Integrating ethical frameworks into machine learning systems requires careful consideration at every stage of development. This section will delve into practical approaches for incorporating ethical standards, such as building fairness metrics into models, conducting comprehensive bias assessments, and ensuring transparency and explainability in algorithmic decision-making.

Ethical Integration in ML Systems

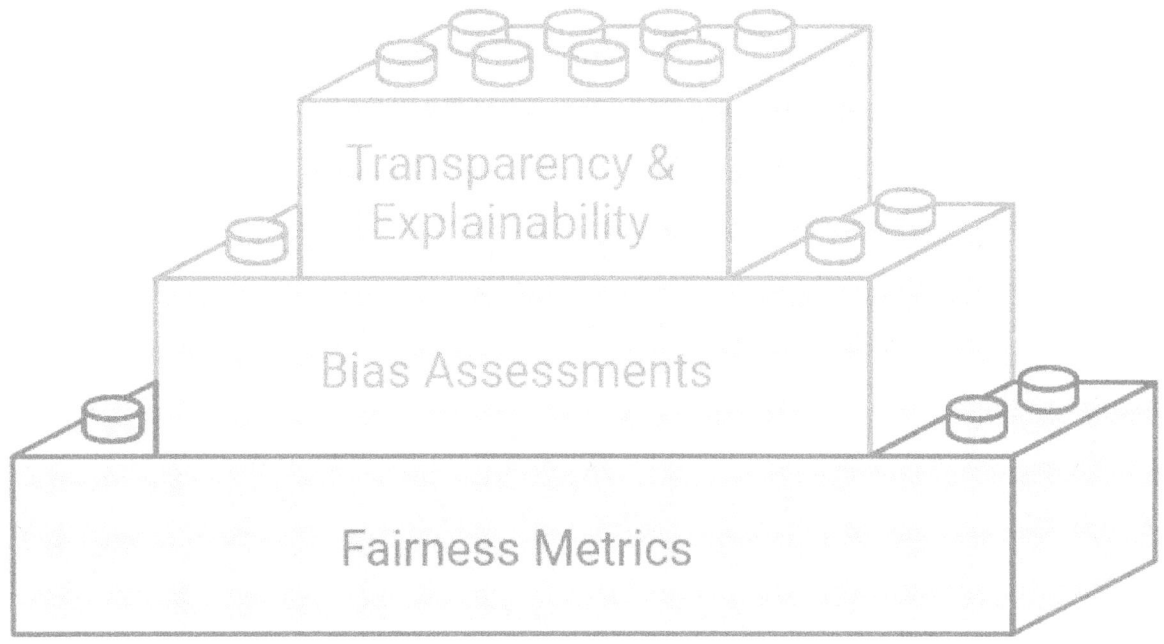

Section 7: Addressing Ethical Challenges in Machine Learning While ethical frameworks provide a guiding light, machine learning presents unique challenges that demand ongoing vigilance. This section will highlight some of the ethical challenges faced in machine learning, including algorithmic biases, unintended consequences, and the potential for discrimination. It will also discuss methods to mitigate these challenges and foster responsible AI development.

How to address ethical challenges in machine learning?

Mitigate Algorithmic Bias

Implementing fairness metrics and bias assessments to ensure equitable outcomes.

Prevent Unintended Consequences

Conducting thorough impact assessments to foresee and address potential issues.

Avoid Discrimination

Establishing guidelines and monitoring systems to prevent biased outcomes.

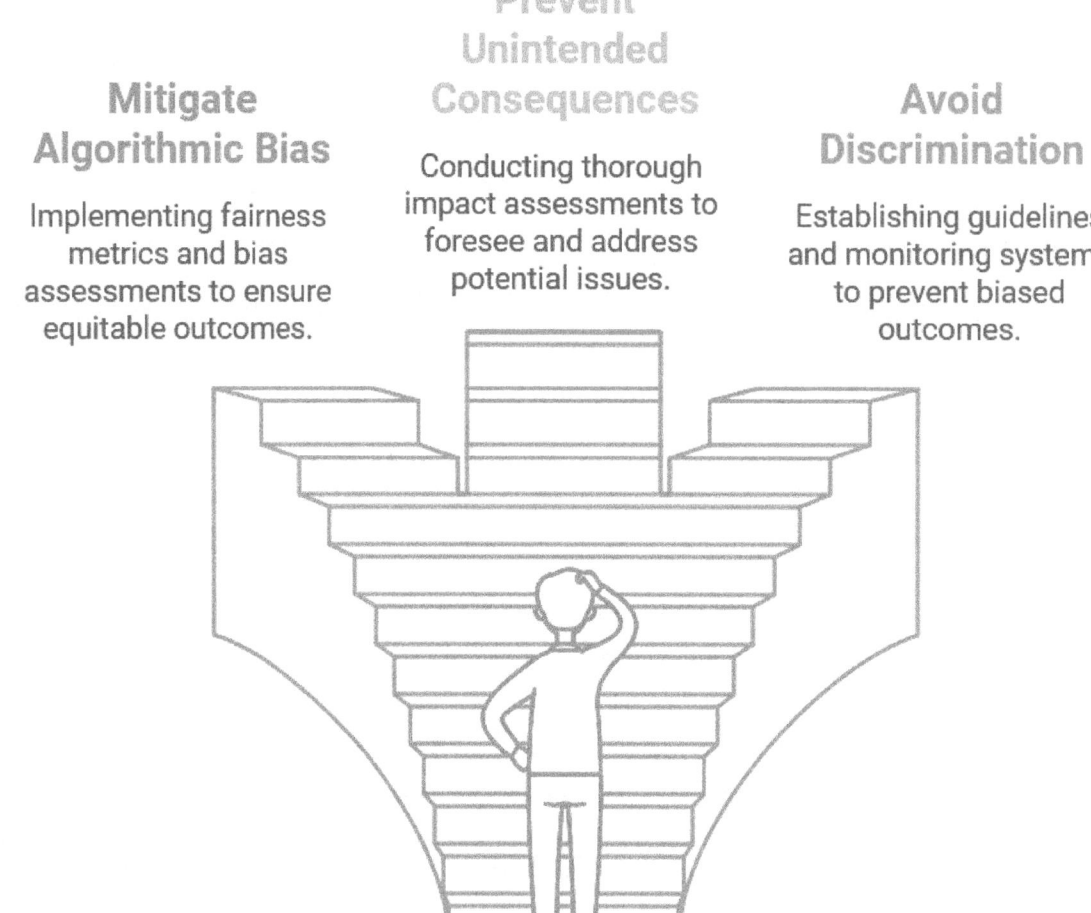

Section 8: Conclusion The application of ethical frameworks in machine learning is instrumental in creating AI systems that align with societal values and respect individual rights. By understanding and leveraging frameworks like utilitarianism, deontological ethics, and virtue ethics, we can foster responsible innovation in the field of machine learning. Embracing ethical considerations is not only essential for addressing potential risks but also for building trust and ensuring the long-term success of AI technologies.

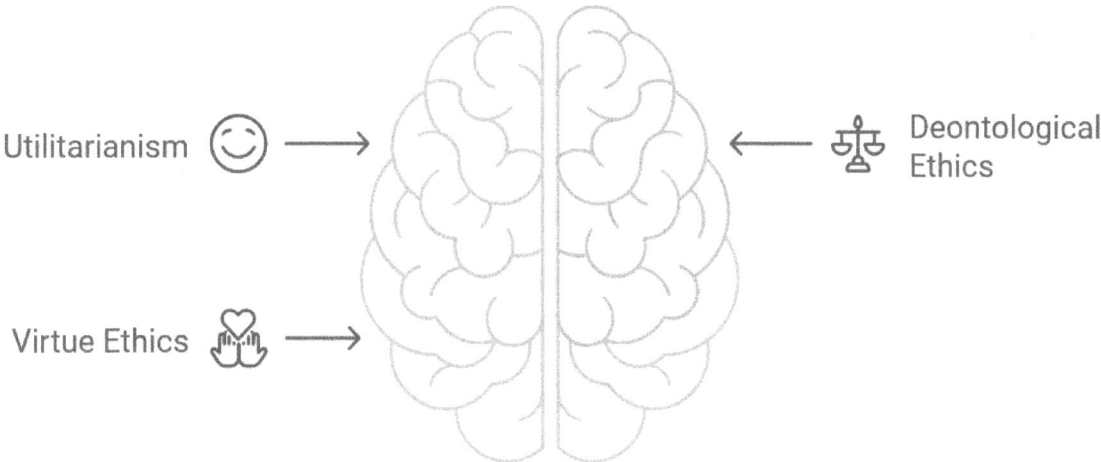

Note:

Ensure to add relevant code snippets, examples, and case studies to illustrate the practical application of ethical frameworks in machine learning throughout the tutorial.

Question 1

What is the key principle of utilitarianism?

1 - To prioritize personal happiness

2 - To maximize overall happiness or well-being for the greatest number of people

3 - To minimize suffering

4 - To pursue individual benefits

The correct answer is number 2

Question 2

What does the Rawlsian justice framework emphasize in machine learning?

1 - Ensuring fairness and equality by minimizing biases and discrimination

2 - Maximizing personal liberty and freedom

3 - Promoting individual happiness and well-being

4 - Protecting privacy and obtaining consent

The correct answer is number 1

Bias and Fairness in Machine Learning

Understanding bias in machine learning

Machine learning algorithms have become incredibly powerful tools, capable of making complex decisions and predictions based on vast amounts of data. However, it is crucial to recognize that these algorithms are not immune to bias. Bias in machine learning refers to the systematic error that creeps into the decision-making process, leading to unfair outcomes or discriminatory treatment of certain individuals or groups.

Bias in Machine Learning Algorithms

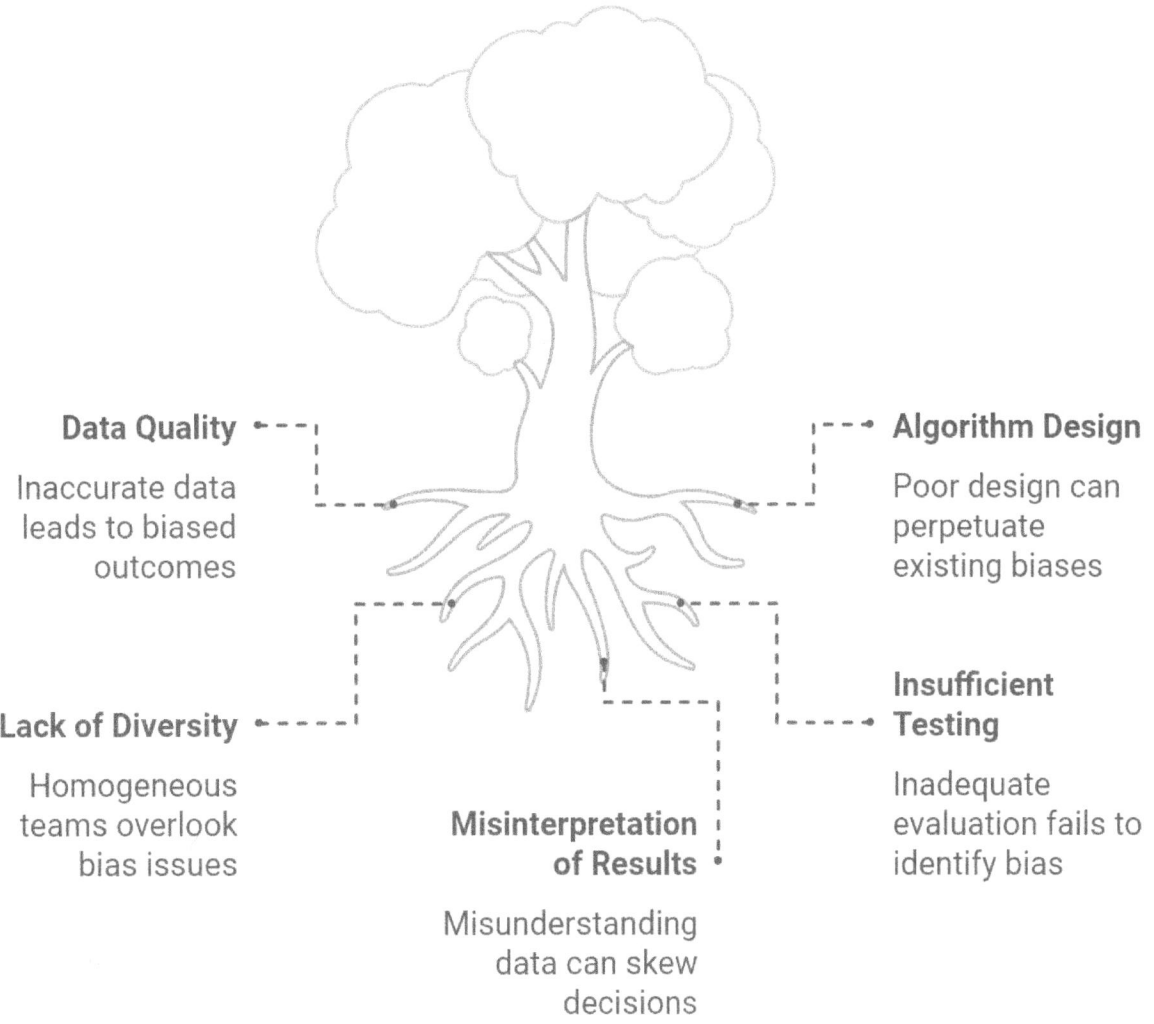

Data Quality — Inaccurate data leads to biased outcomes

Algorithm Design — Poor design can perpetuate existing biases

Lack of Diversity — Homogeneous teams overlook bias issues

Misinterpretation of Results — Misunderstanding data can skew decisions

Insufficient Testing — Inadequate evaluation fails to identify bias

In this tutorial, we will explore the concept of bias and fairness in machine learning and discuss strategies to understand and mitigate these issues. By the end of this tutorial, you will have a solid understanding of the importance of addressing bias in machine learning algorithms and how to ensure fairness in your models.

1. What is Bias in Machine Learning?

- Definition of bias in machine learning.

- Relationship between bias and fairness.

- Examples of bias in different domains (e.g., healthcare, hiring, finance).

Exploring Bias in Machine Learning

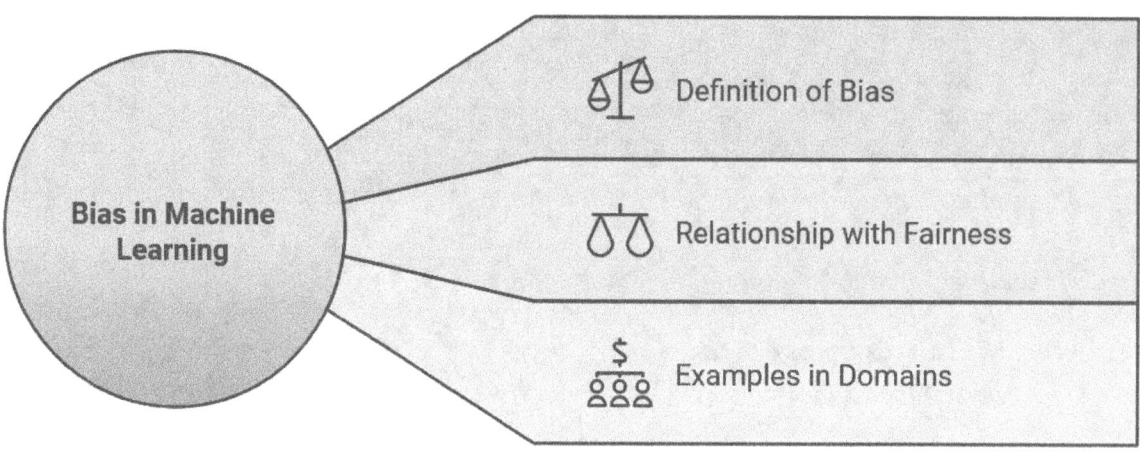

2. Sources of Bias in Machine Learning

- Data collection biases.

- Pre-processing biases.

- Feature biases.

- Algorithmic biases.

- Feedback loop biases.

What are the sources of bias in machine learning?

Data Collection Biases

These biases occur during the gathering of data, leading to unrepresentative datasets.

Pre-processing Biases

Biases introduced during data cleaning and transformation processes.

Feature Biases

Biases arising from the selection and weighting of features in the model.

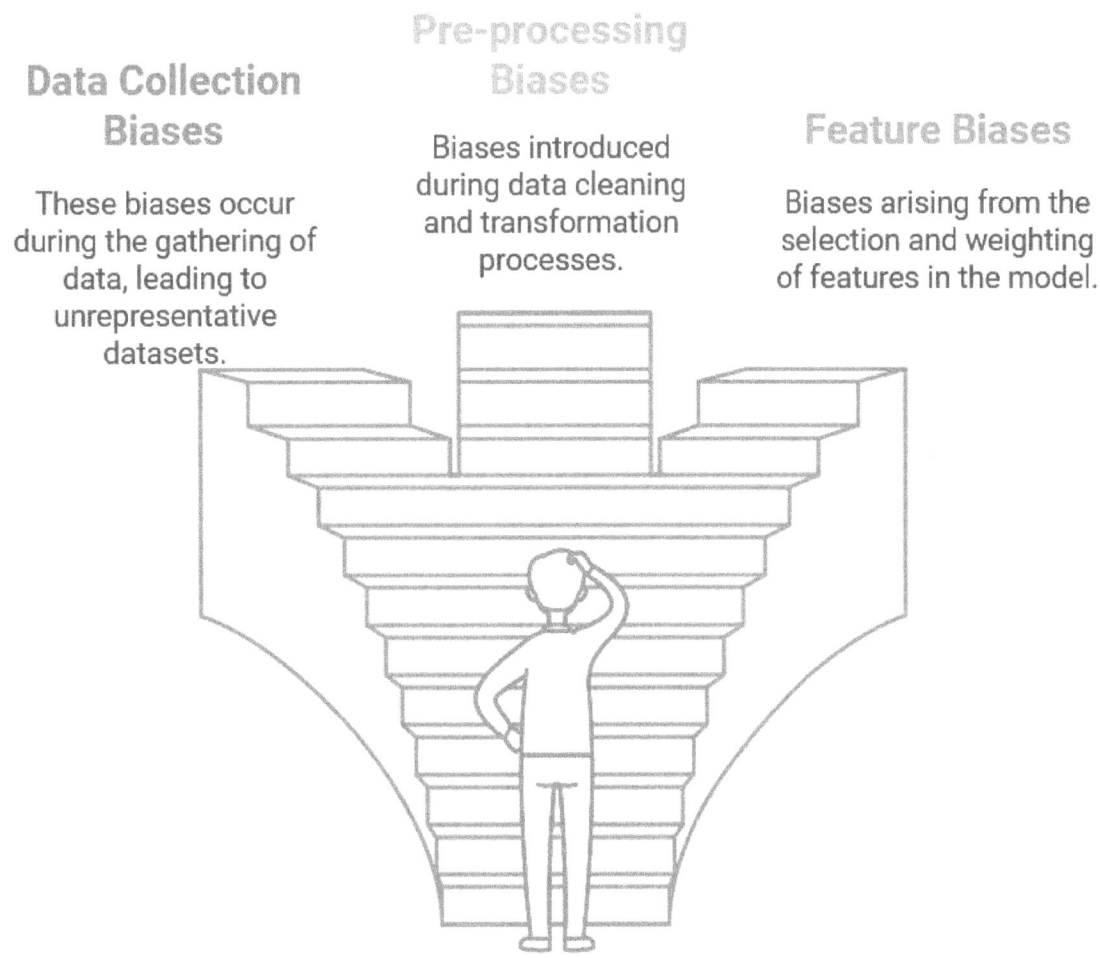

3. Measuring Bias in Machine Learning Algorithms

- Metrics for quantifying bias (e.g., disparate impact, equalized odds, statistical parity).

- Evaluation methods for detecting bias.

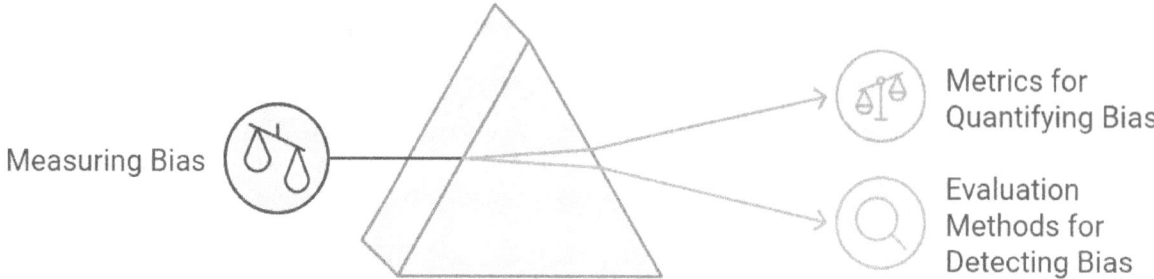

Exploring Bias Measurement in Machine Learning

4. Understanding the Implications of Biased Algorithms

- Harm caused by biased algorithms.

- Negative impacts on disadvantaged groups.

- Legal and ethical considerations.

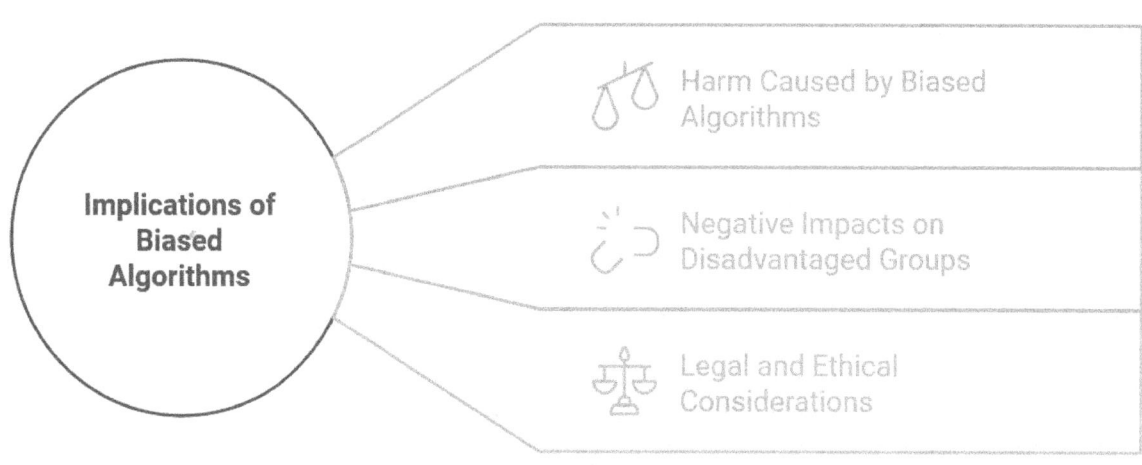

Exploring the Dimensions of Biased Algorithms

5. Mitigating Bias in Machine Learning

- Collecting diverse and representative datasets.

- Pre-processing techniques to minimize bias.

- Feature engineering to reduce bias.

- Algorithmic techniques (e.g., fairness constraints, re-weighting, calibration).

- Regularization methods for fairness.

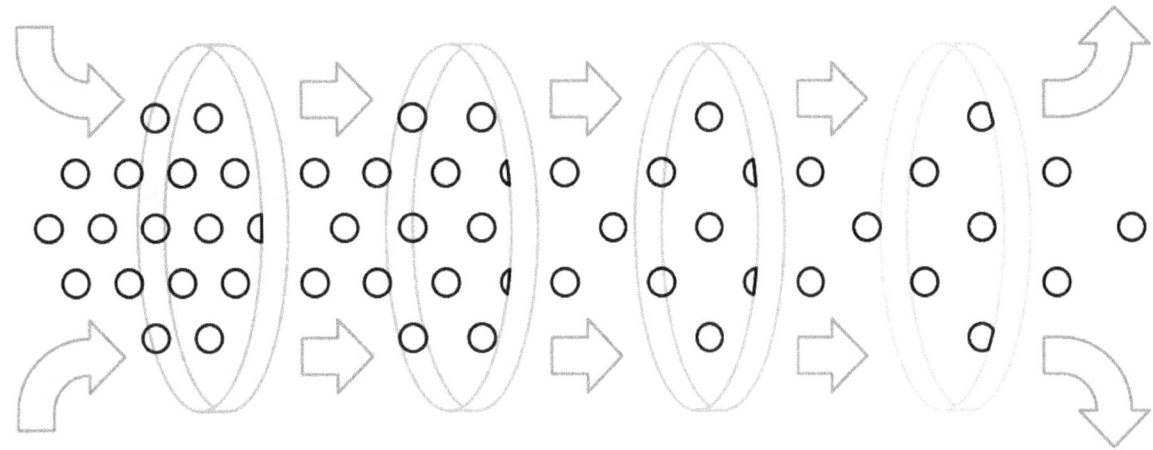

6. Algorithmic Transparency and Interpretability

- The importance of transparency in machine learning algorithms.

- Techniques to interpret and explain model decisions.

- Balancing transparency with privacy concerns.

Lack of transparency hinders understanding and raises privacy concerns.

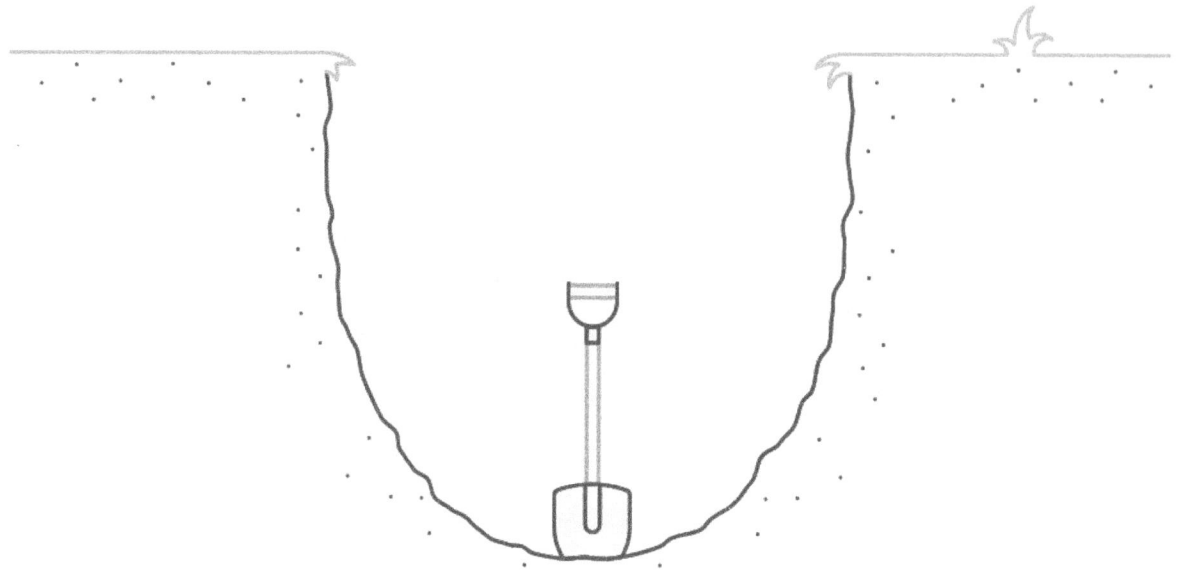

7. Addressing Bias in Real-World Applications

- Case studies of bias in different domains.

- Strategies employed by organizations to tackle bias.

- Regulatory approaches to ensure fairness.

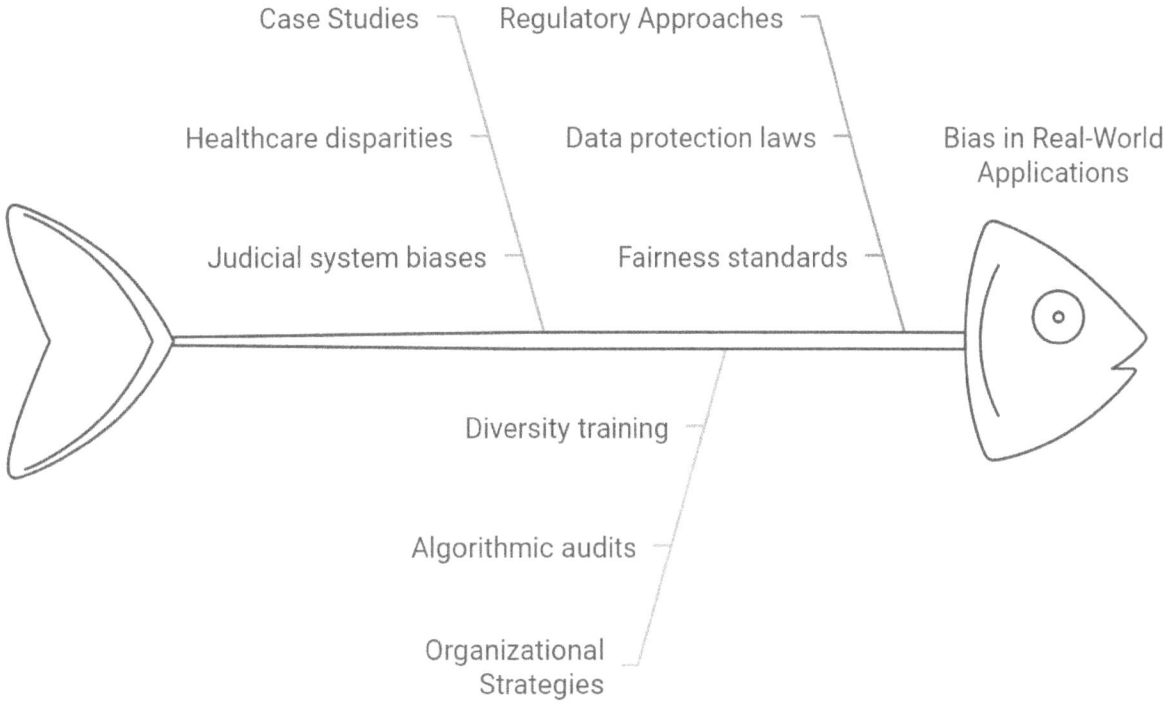

8. Future Directions in Bias and Fairness Research

- State-of-the-art research on bias and fairness.

- Open challenges and areas for improvement.

- Emerging techniques for combating bias.

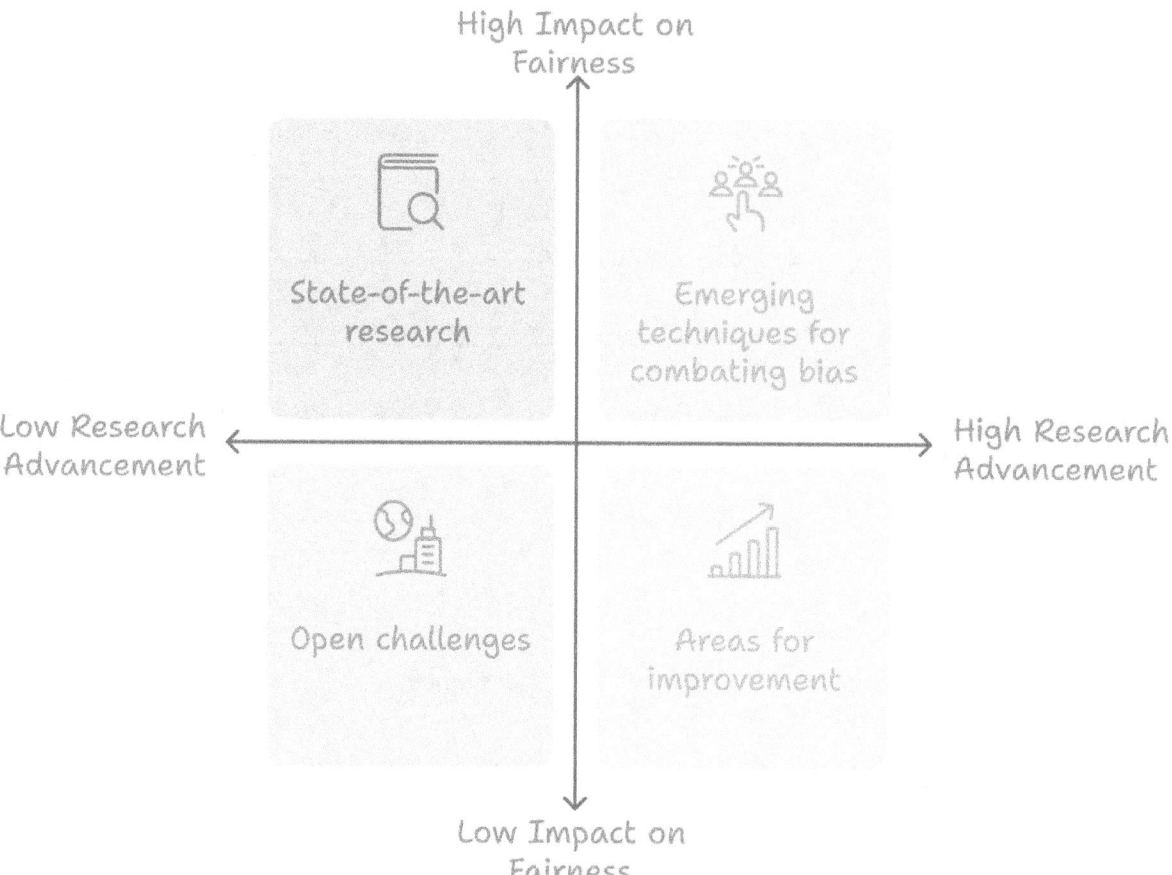

In conclusion, understanding bias in machine learning is crucial to developing fair and ethical algorithms. It is important to recognize that bias can arise from various sources throughout the machine learning pipeline, from data collection to algorithmic decisions. By measuring and mitigating bias, and ensuring transparency and interpretability, we can work towards building more fair and trustworthy machine learning models.

Types of bias

Types of Bias in Machine Learning

Bias and fairness are crucial concepts in machine learning that have a profound impact on the development and deployment of algorithms. Understanding the various types of bias is essential to mitigate unfairness and ensure ethical decision-making. In this tutorial, we will explore different types of bias in the context of bias and fairness in machine learning.

1. Sampling Bias: Sampling bias occurs when the data used to train a machine learning model does not represent the target population accurately. This can lead to biased predictions if the training data is not sufficiently diverse or representative. For example, if a facial recognition system is trained primarily on data from one ethnicity, it may struggle to accurately identify individuals from other ethnicities.

2. Algorithmic Bias: Algorithmic bias refers to the biases inherent in the design and implementation of machine learning algorithms. These biases can emerge due to various factors, such as biased training data, flawed feature selection, or biased assumptions made during the model development process. Algorithmic bias can lead to unequal treatment and unfair outcomes for certain individuals or groups.

Algorithmic Bias in Machine Learning

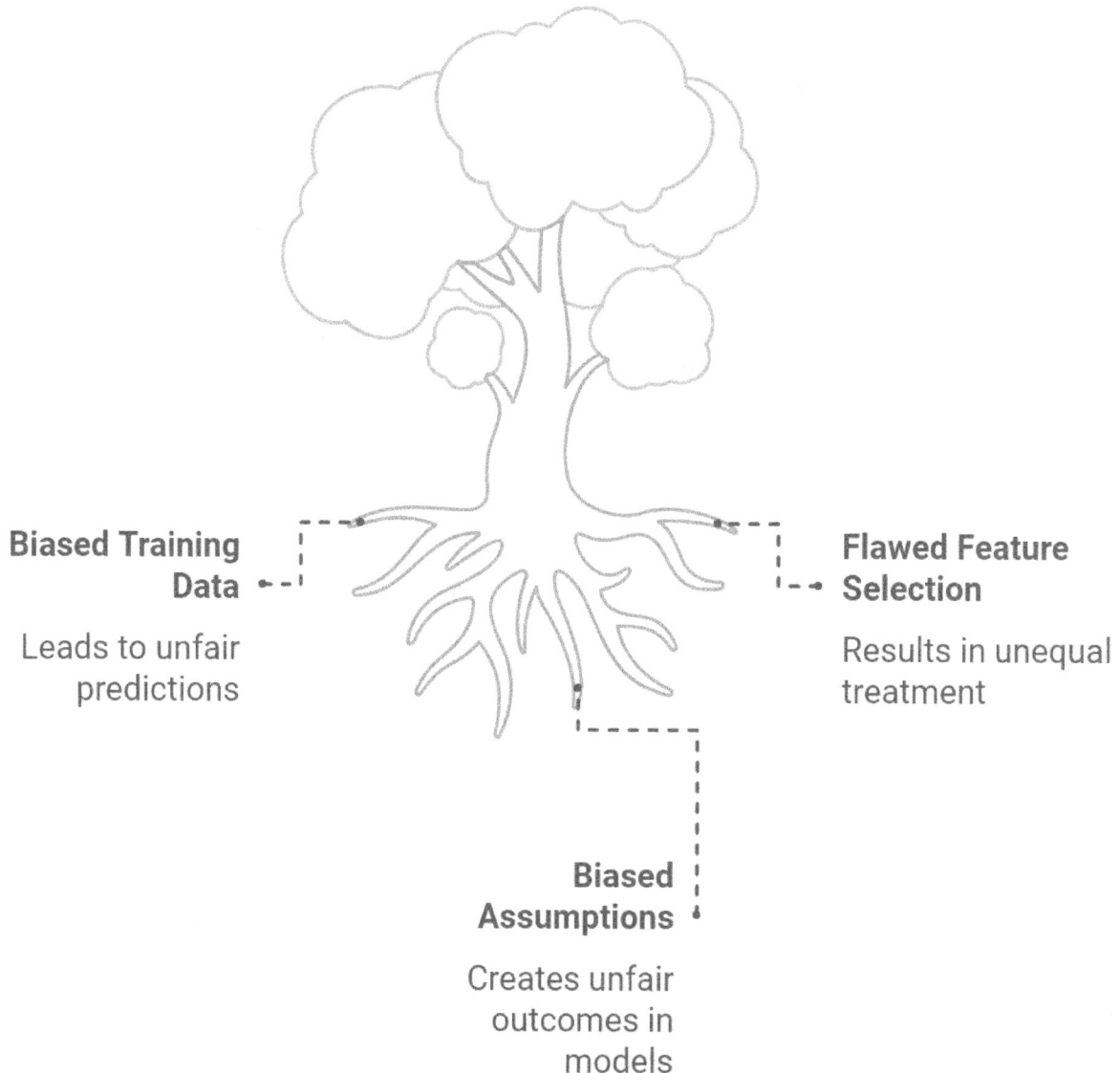

3. Labeling Bias: Labeling bias occurs when the training data used to create a machine learning model contains inaccurate, misleading, or biased labels. This can arise from human annotators' biases, inconsistencies in the labeling process, or reliance on unreliable external sources. Labeling bias can significantly impact the performance and fairness of a model, as the model learns based on the provided labels.

4. Prejudice Bias: Prejudice bias refers to the biases stemming from societal prejudices and systemic discrimination present in the training data. If the training data reflects societal biases, the resulting model may perpetuate and amplify such biases. For instance, if historical loan data exhibits discrimination against certain demographics, a

machine learning model trained on this data may inadvertently deny loans to qualified individuals based on factors like race or gender.

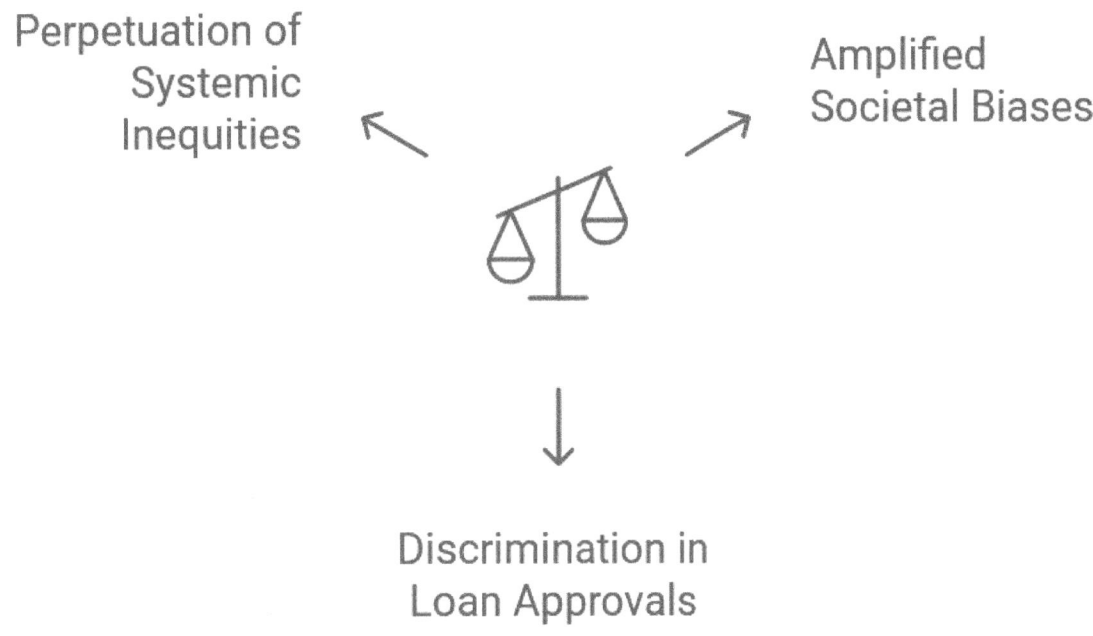

5. Confirmation Bias: Confirmation bias occurs when a machine learning model reinforces existing beliefs or prejudices instead of providing an impartial and unbiased assessment. This bias can emerge when the training data or the learning algorithm favors certain patterns or outcomes that align with prior expectations. Confirmation bias can hinder the discovery of new insights and limit the model's ability to make fair and unbiased predictions.

6. Presentation Bias: Presentation bias arises when the results or outputs of a machine learning model are presented in a manner that may mislead or sway the interpretation of the results. This bias can happen due to selective reporting or cherry-picking results that support a particular narrative. Presentation bias can influence decision-making and exacerbate unfairness if the results are not objectively and transparently communicated.

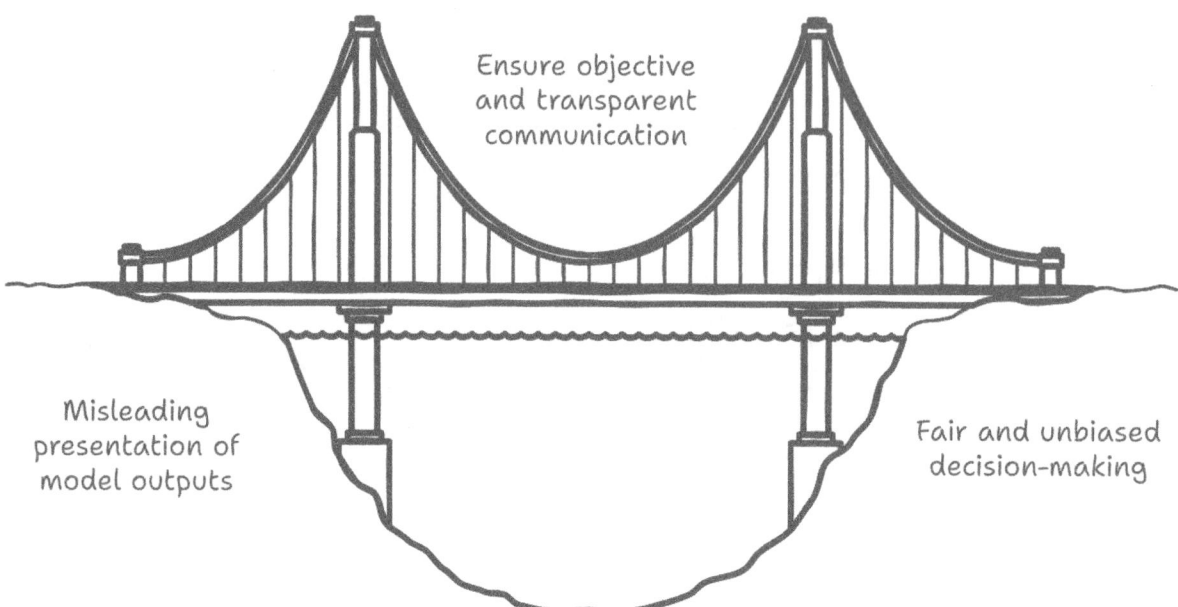

7. Automation Bias: Automation bias refers to the tendency to rely blindly on machine learning models or automation systems without critically evaluating their outputs. This bias can arise when humans trust machine-generated predictions or recommendations without questioning their validity or considering potential biases. Automation bias can lead to uncritical decision-making and the perpetuation of biases present in the models.

8. Temporal Bias: Temporal bias occurs when there are temporal variations in the data used for training and deploying a machine learning model. The biases present in historical data may not accurately reflect the current societal contexts, and the model's outdated knowledge may result in unfair predictions or decisions. Temporal bias emphasizes the importance of continuously updating and reevaluating machine learning models to account for changing dynamics and shifting biases.

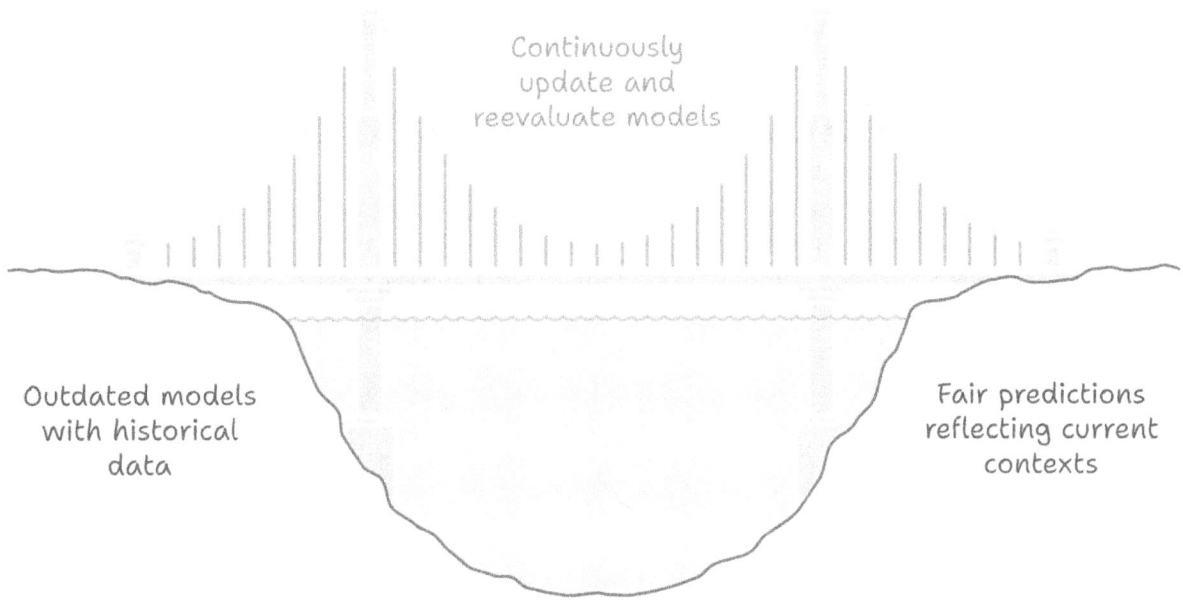

By understanding these different types of bias, we can take proactive steps to mitigate bias and promote fairness in machine learning. Employing diverse and representative training data, implementing bias-aware algorithms, and continuously monitoring and evaluating models can help combat bias and ensure unbiased decision-making in machine learning applications.

Types of Bias and Fairness Concerns in Machine Learning

In the field of artificial intelligence, machine learning algorithms play a crucial role in decision-making processes. However, these algorithms are not exempt from biases. Biases in machine learning can lead to unfair outcomes in various domains such as hiring, lending, and criminal justice. It is essential, therefore, to understand and address these biases to ensure fairness in machine learning.

1. Definition of Bias and Fairness in Machine Learning:

- Bias refers to systematically favoring certain groups or individuals over others.

- Fairness aims to ensure that decision-making processes are unbiased and treat all individuals equitably.

- In the context of machine learning, fairness means eliminating or minimizing both obvious and subtle biases in algorithms.

2. Types of Bias:

Although the topic has already been covered, it's important to have a brief overview of the different types of bias that can occur in machine learning systems:

- Algorithmic Bias: This bias arises from inadequacies in the design or training process of machine learning algorithms.

- Data Bias: Bias can be embedded in the training data itself, leading to discriminatory outcomes in predictions or classifications.

- User Interaction Bias: Biases can result from the way users interact with machine learning systems, either through biased feedback or biased interpretations of output.

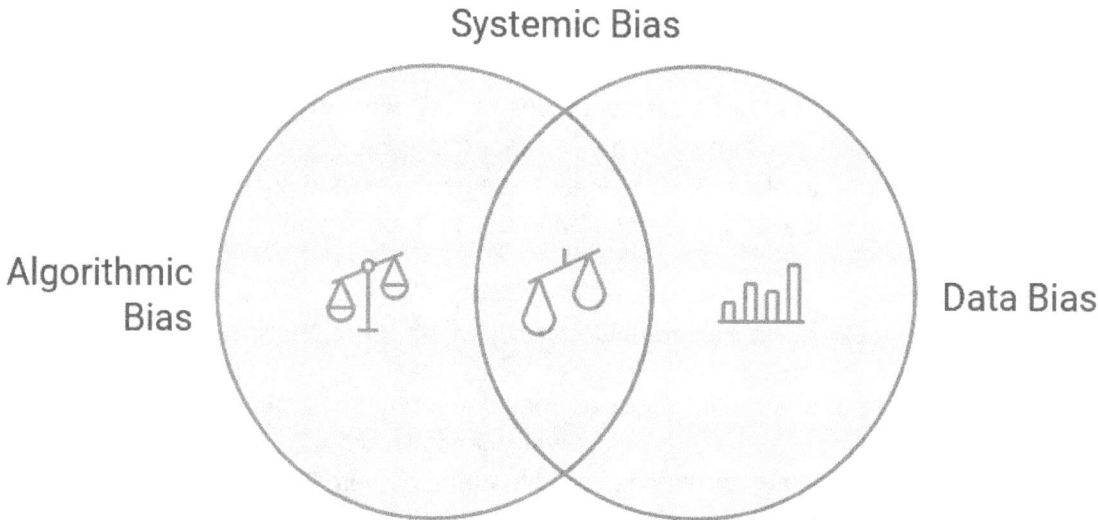

3. Fairness Metrics and Measures:

To detect and mitigate bias in machine learning algorithms, various fairness metrics and measures have been developed. Some of the commonly used metrics include:

- Statistical Parity: It measures the extent to which outcomes differ across different demographic groups.

- Equal Opportunity: This metric focuses on ensuring equal true positive rates across different groups, particularly in classification tasks.

- Predictive Parity: It examines whether the probability of positive outcomes is equal across different groups.

Note: While these metrics are useful, it is important to contextualize them appropriately based on the specific domain and application.

4. Challenges in Achieving Fairness:

Achieving fairness in machine learning is a complex task. Several challenges need to be addressed:

- Data Collection Bias: Biases in historical data can be perpetuated in machine learning algorithms, making it difficult to ensure fairness.

- Trade-offs: Sometimes, optimizing for one fairness metric may be in conflict with another metric, highlighting the need for careful decision-making.

- Model Interpretability: Complex machine learning models can lack interpretability, making it challenging to pinpoint the source of bias.

Challenges in Achieving Fairness in Machine Learning

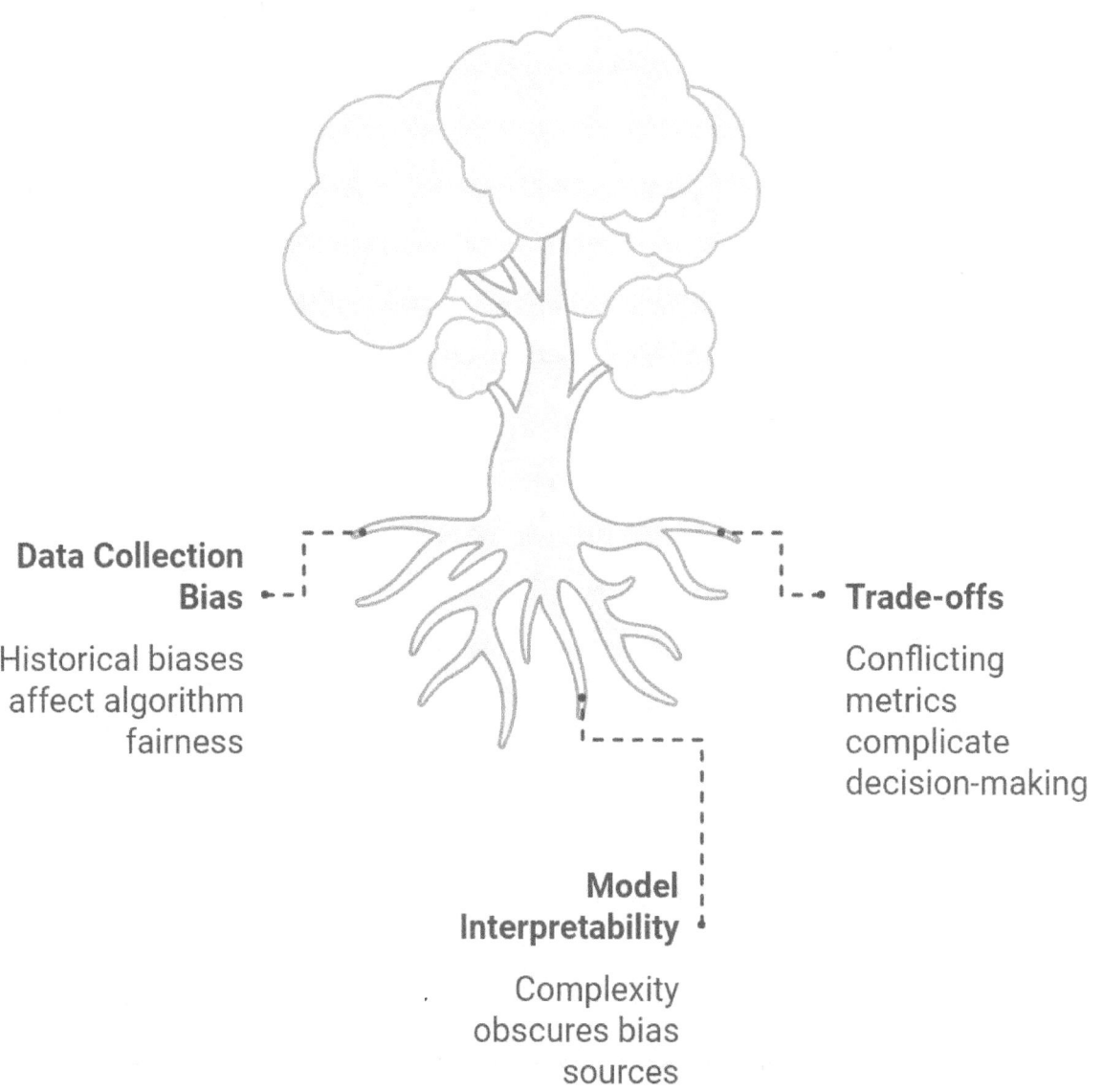

Data Collection Bias

Historical biases affect algorithm fairness

Trade-offs

Conflicting metrics complicate decision-making

Model Interpretability

Complexity obscures bias sources

5. Mitigation Strategies for Bias:

To enhance fairness in machine learning systems, several strategies can be implemented:

- Data Preprocessing: Analyze and preprocess the data to identify and mitigate biases before training the algorithm.

- Algorithmic Adjustments: Incorporate fairness considerations during the training and evaluation of machine learning models.

- Regular Monitoring: Continuously assess and evaluate the model's performance to detect and correct biases that may emerge over time.

Note:

It is important to remember that fairness cannot be achieved by addressing bias alone. Fairness must be integrated into all stages of the machine learning pipeline, from data collection to deployment.

Conclusion:

Ensuring fairness in machine learning is a multidimensional challenge, but one that is crucial to address. By understanding different types of bias, utilizing fairness metrics, and implementing appropriate mitigation strategies, we can work towards creating more equitable machine learning algorithms. Addressing bias and promoting fairness will

ultimately lead to more just outcomes and a responsible and inclusive AI ecosystem.

Algorithmic transparency and interpretability

Algorithmic Transparency and Interpretability with Bias and Fairness in Machine Learning

In the field of machine learning, algorithms are increasingly being used to automate decisions that impact individuals in various domains. However, there is growing concern that these algorithms may exhibit biases that can perpetuate discrimination and unfairness in decision-making processes. To address this, there is a need for algorithmic transparency and interpretability, which allow for understanding and mitigating biases in machine learning models. In this tutorial, we will explore the concepts of algorithmic transparency and interpretability to bias and fairness in machine learning.

1. Overview of Algorithmic Transparency and Interpretability

- Defining algorithmic transparency and interpretability

- Importance of algorithmic transparency and interpretability in machine learning

- How algorithmic transparency and interpretability relate to bias and fairness in machine learning

2. Types of Algorithm Bias

- Understand different types of biases that can be present in machine learning algorithms

- Data bias, model bias, and output bias

- Examples of real-life cases showcasing algorithmic bias and its consequences

3. The Need for Algorithmic Transparency

- Understanding the need for transparency in machine learning algorithms

- Implications of opaque algorithms in decision-making processes

- Ethical considerations of algorithmic opacity and lack of transparency

4. Techniques for Algorithmic Transparency

- Explainability techniques for machine learning algorithms

- Local interpretability methods (e.g., feature importance, rule-based models)

- Global interpretability methods (e.g., LIME, SHAP, model-agnostic techniques)

- Visualizations and tools for understanding and evaluating algorithmic bias

5. Explainable and Interpretable AI Models

- Overview of explainable and interpretable AI models

- Examples of transparent models (e.g., decision trees, linear models)

- Trade-offs between transparency and performance in complex models (e.g., deep learning)

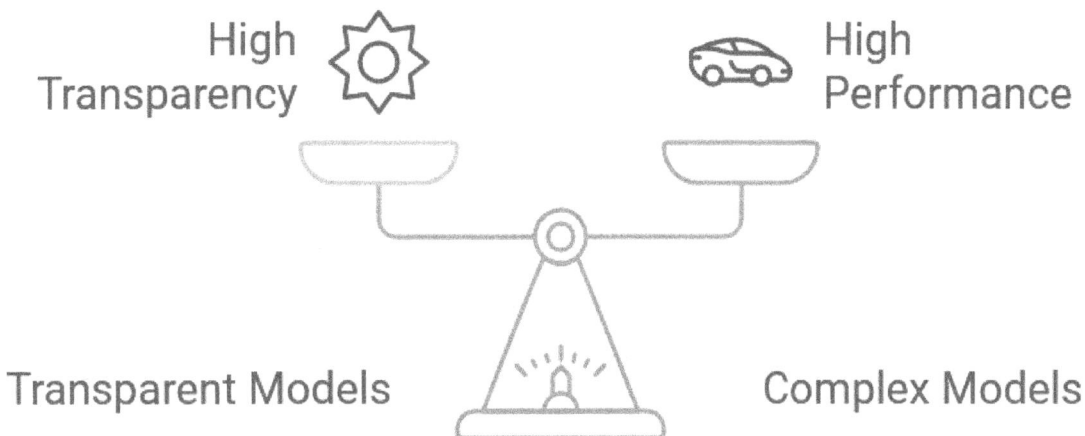

Balancing Transparency and Performance in AI Models

6. Evaluating Bias and Fairness in Machine Learning Models

- Metrics and methods for assessing algorithmic bias and fairness

- Fairness-aware machine learning techniques (e.g., fairness constraints, pre-processing, post-processing)

- Challenges and limitations in evaluating and addressing algorithmic biases

7. Regulatory Frameworks and Ethical Guidelines

- Introduction to regulatory frameworks addressing algorithmic transparency and fairness (e.g., GDPR, AI Ethics Guidelines)

- Discussion on the limitations and challenges in implementing regulatory frameworks

- The role of organizations and researchers in promoting transparency and fairness in algorithms

Exploring Dimensions of Algorithmic Fairness

- Regulatory Frameworks and Ethical Guidelines
- Algorithmic Transparency
- Fairness
- Implementation Challenges
- Role of Organizations and Researchers

8. Case Studies and Real-Life Applications

- Analysis of real-life case studies where algorithmic transparency and interpretability have played a crucial role

- Addressing biases in hiring algorithms, criminal justice systems, and credit scoring systems

9. Future Directions and Open Challenges

- Emerging research and trends in algorithmic transparency and interpretability

- Open challenges in developing transparent and interpretable machine-learning models

- Ethical considerations as machine learning becomes more pervasive

Future Directions in Algorithmic Transparency

Ethical Considerations — Addressing ethical issues as AI becomes more widespread

Algorithmic Transparency — Emerging trends in making algorithms more understandable

Model Interpretability — Challenges in creating models that are easy to interpret

10. Conclusion

- Recap of key concepts in algorithmic transparency and interpretability

- Importance of ensuring fairness and mitigating bias in machine learning algorithms

- Encouragement to further explore and contribute to the field of algorithmic transparency and interpretability

By understanding algorithmic transparency and interpretability with bias and fairness in machine learning, we can strive to build more ethically sound and transparent machine learning models that minimize bias and promote fairness in decision-making processes.

Question 1

What are the types of algorithm bias?

1 - Data bias, model bias, and output bias

2 - Sampling bias, algorithmic bias, and labeling bias

3 - Prejudice bias, confirmation bias, and presentation bias

4 - Automation bias, temporal bias, and fairness bias

The answer is number 1

Question 2

What is algorithmic transparency and interpretability?

1 - Understanding and mitigating biases in machine learning models

2 - Explaining the concepts of ethically sound machine learning

3 - Measuring fairness and equality in algorithmic decision-making

4 - Discussing the implications of bias in machine learning

The answer is number 1

Data Privacy and Security

Importance of data privacy in machine learning

Protecting data privacy is crucial in the field of machine learning. As machine learning algorithms rely heavily on large datasets, it is essential to prioritize the security and privacy of the data being used. In this tutorial, we will delve into the importance of data privacy in machine learning and explore various aspects of ensuring data privacy and security.

1. Understanding Data Privacy:

- Define data privacy and its significance in the context of machine learning.

- Explain the potential risks and consequences associated with data breaches and unauthorized access to sensitive information.

2. Legal and Ethical Considerations:

- Discuss the importance of adhering to data protection regulations such as the General Data Protection Regulation (GDPR).

- Highlight the ethical considerations related to data privacy and machine learning, including bias and discrimination.

Legal and Ethical Data Privacy

Bias and Discrimination
Addressing and mitigating unfair treatment in data practices.

GDPR Compliance
Ensuring adherence to international data protection standards.

Ethical Data Use
Promoting fairness and transparency in data handling.

3. Data Anonymization Techniques (Review):

- Briefly mention prominent techniques for data anonymization, such as k-anonymity and differential privacy.

- Reference existing tutorial(s) on the topic and encourage the readers to explore those resources.

4. Securing Machine Learning Models and Data (Review):

- Highlight the significance of securing machine learning models and the data they operate on.

- Reference existing tutorial(s) on securing machine learning models and data and urge the readers to refer to those resources.

5. Importance of Data Minimization:

- Explain the principle of data minimization and its importance in reducing privacy risks.

- Discuss techniques like data sampling and noise addition that can help minimize the amount of sensitive information stored and processed.

6. Encryption and Secure Data Transmission:

- Introduce the concept of encryption and its role in protecting data privacy.

- Discuss techniques like end-to-end encryption, secure sockets layer (SSL), and secure file transfer protocol (SFTP) for secure data transmission.

7. Access Control and Authorization:

- Explain the significance of access control mechanisms in limiting data access to authorized individuals.

- Discuss techniques like role-based access control (RBAC) and multi-factor authentication (MFA) to enhance data security.

8. Data Storage and Infrastructure Security:

- Highlight the importance of secure data storage practices, including the use of encryption, firewalls, and intrusion detection systems (IDS).

- Discuss the need for regularly updating and patching infrastructure components to mitigate security vulnerabilities.

9. Data De-identification:

- Describe techniques such as anonymization, pseudonymization, and de-identification for reducing the risk of re-identification.

- Discuss the limitations and challenges associated with data de-identification.

10. Model Explainability and Transparency:

- Emphasize the importance of model explainability and transparency to ensure accountability and trust.

- Discuss techniques like interpretable machine learning and model-agnostic methods to improve model explainability.

11. Education and Training:

- Highlight the significance of educating and training individuals involved in machine learning projects about data privacy best practices.

- Encourage readers to stay up-to-date with the latest data privacy and security developments.

12. Conclusion:

- Recap the importance of data privacy in machine learning.

- Reinforce the key concepts discussed throughout the tutorial.

- Encourage readers to prioritize data privacy and security in their machine-learning endeavors.

Remember to continuously emphasize the significance of data privacy in machine learning throughout the tutorial, and provide practical suggestions and examples whenever possible.

Data protection regulations (e.g., GDPR)

Data Protection Regulations (e.g., GDPR) about Data Privacy and Security

1. Understanding the Basics of Data Protection Regulations (e.g., GDPR)

- Definition of data protection regulations

- Why data protection regulations are important for data privacy and security

2. Introduction to GDPR

- What is GDPR?

- A brief history of GDPR

- Scope and applicability of GDPR

3. Key Principles of GDPR

- Lawfulness, fairness, and transparency of data processing

- Purpose limitation and data minimization

- Accuracy and storage limitation of personal data

- Integrity and confidentiality of personal data

- Accountability and transparency

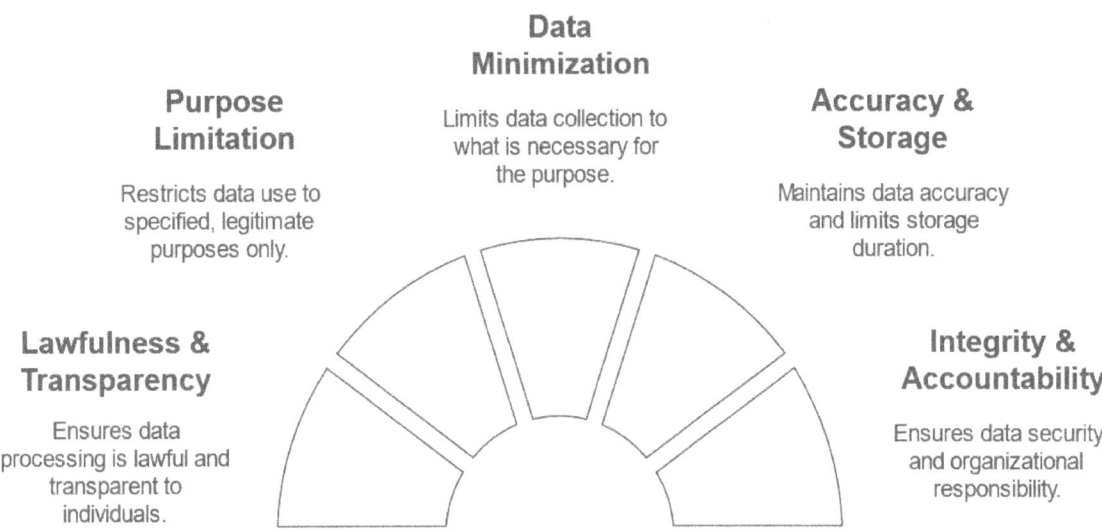

4. Individuals' Rights under GDPR

- Right to be informed

- Right to access personal data

- Right to rectification and erasure

- Right to restrict processing

- Right to data portability

- Right to object

- Rights related to automated decision-making and profiling

5. GDPR Compliance for Organizations

- Data protection officers (DPOs)

- Data protection impact assessments (DPIAs)

- Data processing agreements (DPAs)

- Privacy by design and by default

- Data breach notification requirements

- Cross-border data transfers and adequacy decisions

6. GDPR Enforcement and Penalties

- How GDPR is enforced

- Role of supervisory authorities

- Penalties for non-compliance

- Case studies on GDPR penalties and fines

7. International Data Transfers under GDPR

- Transfer mechanisms for personal data outside the EU

- Standard Contractual Clauses (SCCs)

- Binding Corporate Rules (BCRs)

- EU-US Privacy Shield

8. Challenges and Considerations in Implementing GDPR

- Legal challenges and interpretations of GDPR

- Practical considerations for organizations

- Impact on cross-border data transfers

- Compliance challenges for small businesses and startups

9. Recent Developments and Future of GDPR

- GDPR and emerging technologies (e.g., AI, IoT)

- Potential amendments and updates to GDPR

- Global adoption of GDPR-inspired regulations

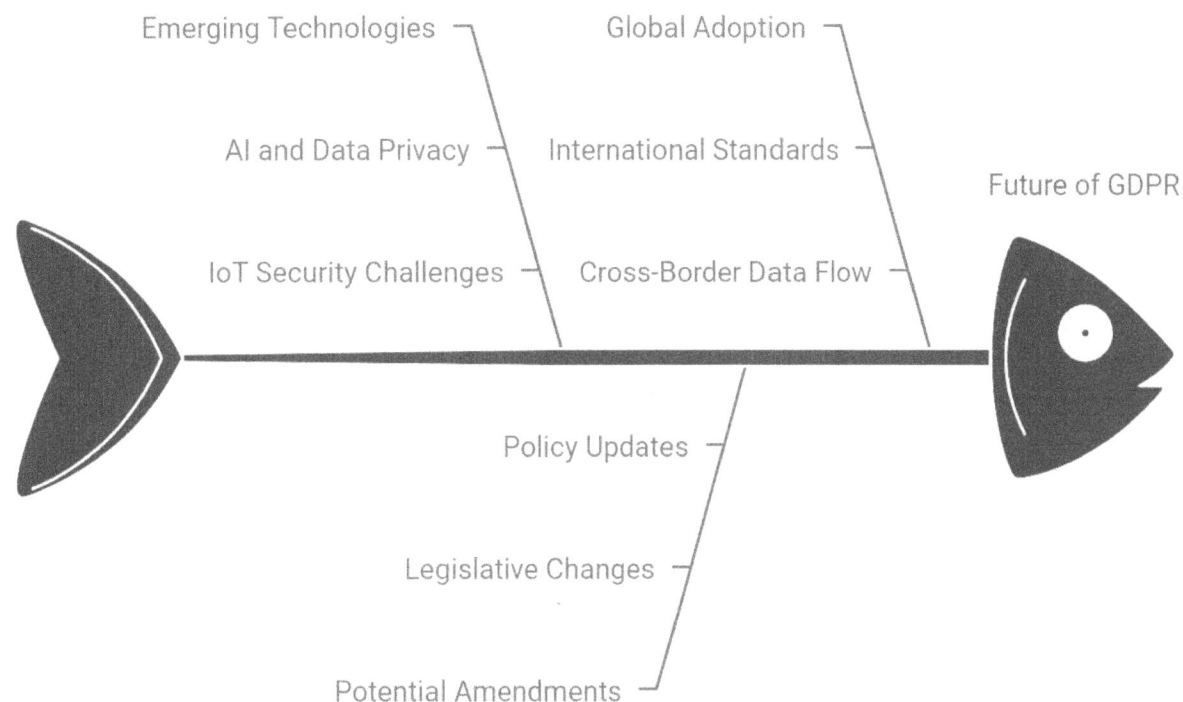

10. Conclusion

- Recap of key points covered in the tutorial

- Importance of data protection regulations for data privacy and security

- Encouragement to stay updated and compliant with GDPR

Remember to always consult legal professionals or seek expert advice to ensure accuracy and compliance with data protection regulations in your specific jurisdiction.

Data anonymization techniques

Ensuring data privacy and security is of utmost importance in today's digital world. With the ever-increasing amount of data being collected and analyzed, organizations need to adopt techniques to protect sensitive information. Data anonymization is one such technique that allows organizations to protect privacy while still utilizing data for analysis and research purposes. In this tutorial, we will explore various data anonymization techniques and their role in data privacy and security.

1. Introduction to Data Anonymization:

- Understanding the importance of data privacy and security.

- Overview of data anonymization as a technique to protect sensitive information.

- How data anonymization facilitates data analysis while preserving privacy.

2. Types of Data Anonymization Techniques:

a. Generalization:

- Exploring the concept of generalization in data anonymization.

- How generalization helps in reducing the granularity of data.

- Examples of generalization techniques, such as numerical range generalization and data truncation.

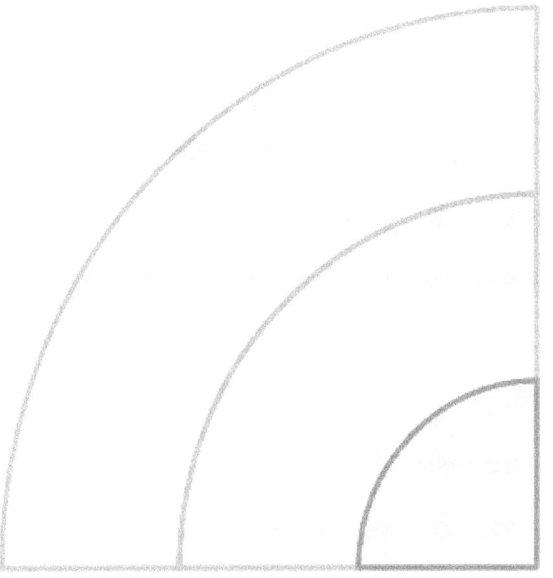

Data Anonymization Techniques

- Techniques
- Reducing Granularity
- Generalization

b. Suppression:

- Understanding suppression as a technique to remove highly identifying data.

- How suppression preserves the overall structure and characteristics of the dataset.

- Examples of suppression techniques, such as k-anonymity and l-diversity.

c. Perturbation:

- Introducing perturbation as a technique to alter data values while preserving statistical properties.

- How perturbation protects privacy by introducing noise.

- Examples of perturbation techniques, such as adding Laplacian noise and implementing differential privacy.

d. Tokenization:

- Exploring tokenization as a technique to replace sensitive data with non-sensitive tokens.

- How tokenization maintains data utility while preserving privacy.

- Examples of tokenization techniques, such as anonymizing credit card numbers and personal identifications.

3. Data Privacy and Security Considerations:

a. Re-identification Attacks:

- Discussing re-identification attacks and their potential impact on privacy.

- Understanding the concept of re-identification risk.

- Techniques to mitigate re-identification risks, such as k-anonymity and differential privacy.

b. Utility-Preserving Techniques:

- Exploring the trade-off between privacy and data utility.

- Understanding how anonymization techniques impact the quality of analysis results.

- Techniques to balance privacy requirements with data utility, such as data de-duplication and query-based anonymization.

c. Legal and Ethical Considerations:

- Discussing the legal and ethical implications of data anonymization.

- Overview of data protection regulations, such as GDPR (General Data Protection Regulation).

- Compliance and best practices for organizations handling sensitive data.

4. Implementing Data Anonymization Techniques:

a. Choosing the Right Anonymization Technique:

- Factors to consider when selecting an appropriate anonymization technique.

- Evaluating the trade-offs between different techniques in terms of privacy and utility.

- Case studies and real-world examples of organizations implementing anonymization techniques.

b. Data Anonymization Tools and Frameworks:

- Overview of popular open-source and commercial tools for data anonymization.

- Comparison of different tools based on features, compatibility, and ease of use.

- Step-by-step guide on how to use a chosen data anonymization tool.

5. Evaluating the Effectiveness of Data Anonymization:

- Understanding the metrics and techniques for evaluating anonymized datasets.

- Overview of approaches, such as information loss measurement and privacy risk assessment.

- Case studies and examples of evaluating the effectiveness of data anonymization techniques.

6. Conclusion:

- Recap of the importance of data privacy and security in today's digital landscape.

- Summary of different data anonymization techniques and their role in protecting privacy.

- Final thoughts on incorporating data anonymization as a best practice for organizations.

By implementing data anonymization techniques, organizations can strike a balance between data privacy and utility. This tutorial has covered various anonymization techniques, their implementation, and the associated considerations. With this knowledge, organizations can protect sensitive information while still leveraging data for analysis and research purposes, ultimately ensuring data privacy and security in an increasingly data-driven world.

Securing machine learning models and data

Securing Machine Learning Models and Data

Machine learning has become increasingly prevalent in various industries, enabling organizations to make data-driven decisions and gain valuable insights. However, with the growing reliance on machine learning algorithms, it is crucial to ensure the security and privacy of both the models and the data they work with. In this tutorial, we will explore different strategies and techniques for securing machine learning models and data.

1. Threat Modeling:

- Begin by conducting a comprehensive threat modeling exercise to identify potential risks and vulnerabilities related to your machine learning system. Consider internal and external threats, such as unauthorized access, malicious attacks, or insider threats.

- Evaluate the potential impact of these threats on your models and data, and prioritize them based on their severity. This step will help you design appropriate security measures based on the identified risks.

2. Secure Data Storage:

- Implement robust data storage practices to protect sensitive information. Apply encryption mechanisms, both at rest and in transit, to safeguard data from unauthorized access. Use strong encryption algorithms and ensure proper key management.

- Regularly back up your data and consider implementing off-site storage to mitigate the risk of data loss or breaches. Monitor access to stored data and implement access controls to restrict unauthorized access.

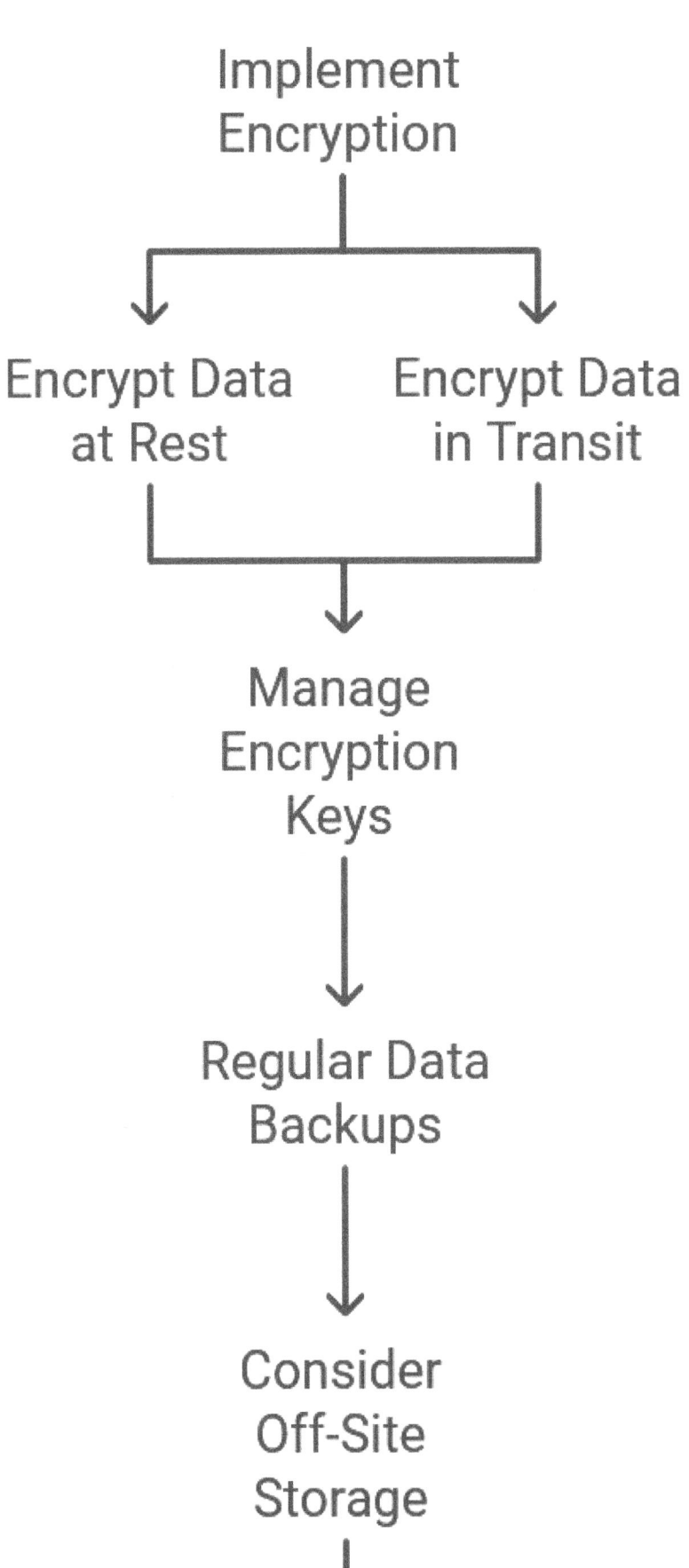

3. Secure Data Processing:

- Protect data during the preprocessing phase by following best practices. Ensure the confidentiality, integrity, and availability of data while in transit and at rest. Implement encryption and hash functions to protect against tampering or unauthorized modifications.

- Implement secure coding practices to prevent security vulnerabilities in your machine learning code. Regularly assess and test the code for potential weaknesses, and apply patches or updates promptly.

4. Secure Model Training:

- Implement access controls and authentication mechanisms to restrict access to machine learning systems and models. Grant appropriate privileges based on the principle of least privilege, ensuring that only authorized personnel can access and modify the models.

- Regularly review and update access controls to align with changes in your organization's personnel and needs. Monitor and log any model modifications or changes made during training.

5. Secure Model Deployment:

- When deploying machine learning models, consider the security implications. Implement secure deployment practices, such as containerization or virtualization, to isolate and protect models from potential attacks.

- Continuous monitoring and logging of the deployed models can help detect any anomalous behavior or potential security breaches. Implement robust intrusion detection and prevention mechanisms to safeguard the models from attacks.

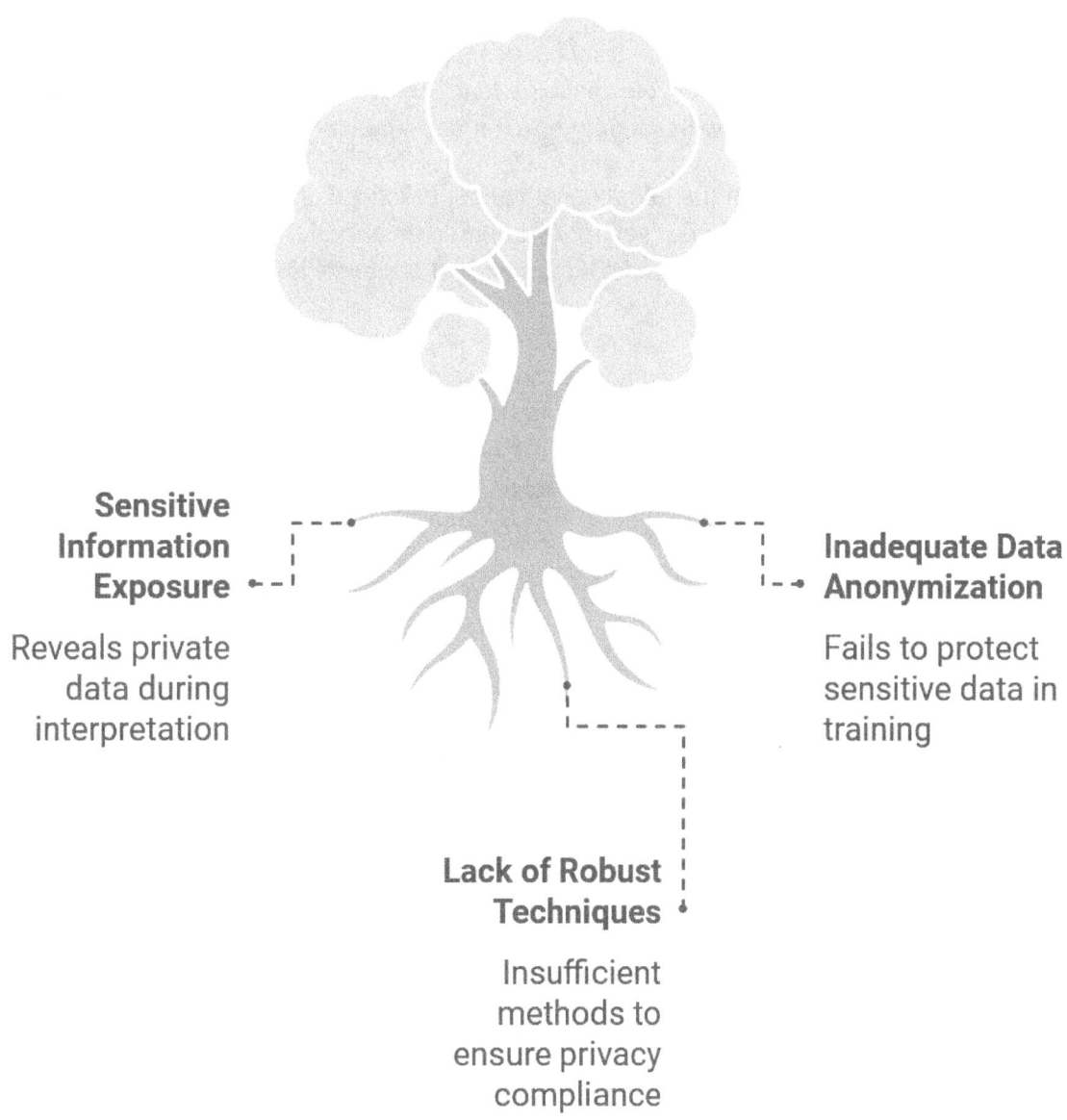

6. Model Interpretability and Privacy:

Model interpretability is crucial, but it can pose privacy risks if sensitive information is revealed. To balance interpretability and privacy concerns, apply techniques such as differential privacy, federated learning, or homomorphic encryption.

- Ensure that sensitive data is anonymized or redacted before using it to train models. Consider using synthetic data generation methods that retain important statistical properties without exposing sensitive information.

7. Ongoing Security Maintenance:

- Implement regular vulnerability assessments and penetration testing to identify potential security weaknesses in your machine learning systems. Conduct periodic audits to ensure compliance with security policies and regulations.

- Stay updated with the latest security best practices, industry standards, and privacy regulations to adapt your security measures as needed. Regularly patch or update your machine learning frameworks, libraries, and dependencies to address any known vulnerabilities.

By following the strategies and techniques outlined in this tutorial, you can enhance the security and privacy of your machine-learning models and data. Remember that data privacy and security should be an ongoing effort, requiring continuous monitoring and improvement to keep pace with evolving threats.

Question 1

What are the key principles of GDPR?

1 - Lawfulness, fairness, and transparency of data processing

2 - Purpose limitation and data minimization

3 - Accuracy and storage limitation of personal data

4 - Integrity and confidentiality of personal data

The right answer is number 4

Question 2

What is GDPR?

1 -General Data Protection Regulation

2 - Global Data Privacy Regulation

3 - General Data Privacy Rules

4 - Global Data Protection Regulation

The right answer is number 1

Ethical responsibility of AI developers

Developing artificial intelligence (AI) systems comes with a significant ethical responsibility. In this tutorial, we will explore the ethical responsibilities that AI developers should uphold when creating AI systems. Specifically, we will focus on the accountability and responsibility that AI developers need to consider throughout the development process. By following these guidelines, AI developers can ensure that the AI systems they create are trustworthy, fair, and align with ethical principles.

1. Understand the Impact of AI Systems:
AI developers need to have a deep understanding of the potential impact their systems can have on various stakeholders, including individuals, organizations, and society as a whole. It is crucial to anticipate the potential consequences, both positive and negative, of the AI system's actions.

2. Consider Fairness and Bias:
AI systems should be designed to be fair and unbiased. Developers must thoroughly evaluate and mitigate any biases that may exist in the training data, algorithmic design, or decision-making process. This includes addressing issues related to race, gender, age, and other protected characteristics, which could result in discriminatory outcomes.

3. Ensure Transparency:
Developers should strive for transparency in the design and development of AI systems. Transparency enables external examination of the system's inner workings and decision-making

processes. By providing explanations and justifications for the system's actions, developers can build trust and accountability.

4. Safeguard Privacy and Data Protection:
AI developers must prioritize the privacy and data protection of individuals. Data collection, storage, and usage should follow established privacy regulations. Furthermore, developers should adopt measures that prevent unauthorized access or misuse of any personal or sensitive data.

5. Develop Explainable AI:
While AI systems can be immensely complex, developers should strive to build explainable AI. This means ensuring that the decisions made by the system can be understood, justified, and explained in human-understandable terms. Explainability enhances trust and allows for appropriate human intervention when necessary.

6. Consider Societal Impact:
AI developers should assess the societal impact of their systems. This involves considering the potential economic, social, and cultural consequences that AI can have on individuals and communities. Developers should work in collaboration with stakeholders to identify and mitigate any negative impacts that may arise.

7. Establish Accountability Mechanisms:
AI developers should establish accountability mechanisms to ensure proper oversight and responsibility for the AI systems they create. This may involve defining clear lines of responsibility, creating reporting mechanisms for unintended consequences, and implementing feedback loops for continuous improvement.

8. Engage in Continuous Learning:
To remain ethically responsible, AI developers should actively engage in continuous learning and stay updated with advancements in ethics, regulations, and best practices related to AI development. This allows

developers to adapt their practices and incorporate new insights to ensure ongoing ethical responsibility.

Ensuring accountability in machine learning

The field of artificial intelligence (AI) has seen remarkable advancements in recent years, particularly in the area of machine learning. Machine learning algorithms are now being used to automate decision-making processes in a wide range of domains, from healthcare to finance. However, as AI systems become more sophisticated, there is an increasing need to ensure accountability and responsibility in their usage. In this tutorial, we will explore the importance of accountability in machine learning and discuss strategies to achieve it.

1. Understanding Accountability in Machine Learning:

    - Define accountability in the context of machine learning.

    - Explain the need for accountability in AI systems.

    - Discuss the potential consequences of unchecked AI decision-making.

2. Principles of Accountability in Machine Learning:

    - Highlight the key principles of accountability in the context of AI systems.

    - Discuss transparency and explain the importance of understanding how AI systems arrive at their decisions.

    - Address the concept of explainability, i.e., the ability to interpret and provide justifications for AI decisions.

3. Evaluating Algorithmic Bias:

    - Explain algorithmic bias and its implications.

    - Discuss the role of bias in machine learning algorithms.

    - Present different methods to detect and mitigate algorithmic bias.

4. Assessing the Ethical Implications of AI Systems:

   - Discuss the ethical challenges posed by AI systems.

   - Explain the potential harm caused by biased or unfair AI decisions.

   - Address the importance of fairness, equity, and inclusivity in AI systems.

5. Implementing Accountability Measures:

   - Explain the concept of Ethical Governance Frameworks and their role in ensuring accountability.

   - Discuss the importance of collaboration between AI developers, stakeholders, and end-users.

   - Present guidelines for designing, developing, and deploying AI systems that prioritize accountability.

6. Auditing and Monitoring AI Systems:

   - Discuss the significance of auditing and monitoring AI systems.

   - Explain the process of conducting audits to identify biases, errors, and potential issues.

   - Highlight the role of ongoing monitoring to ensure continuous accountability.

7. Incorporating Human Oversight:

   - Explore the importance of human oversight in AI decision-making.

   - Discuss the role of human experts in evaluating, validating, and interpreting AI decisions.

   - Address the potential challenges and limitations of human oversight.

8. Educating and Empowering Users:

   - Emphasize the importance of educating users about AI systems.

- Discuss the need for transparency and user awareness of AI decision-making processes.

- Provide strategies for empowering users to understand and challenge AI decisions.

9. Addressing Legal and Regulatory Frameworks:

- Explain the role of legal and regulatory frameworks in ensuring accountability.

- Discuss relevant laws and regulations related to AI and machine learning.

- Address the challenges in developing effective legal and regulatory frameworks for AI systems.

10. Case Studies:

- Provide real-world examples illustrating the importance of accountability in AI systems.

- Discuss how accountability was achieved or the consequences of its absence.

In conclusion, accountability is a crucial aspect of machine learning and AI systems. It ensures that AI decisions are fair, transparent, and aligned with ethical standards. By following the principles of accountability, implementing measures such as auditing and human oversight, and educating users, we can foster responsible and accountable AI systems.

Conclusion:
In this tutorial, we have explored the ethical responsibilities that AI developers should uphold. By considering the impact of AI systems, ensuring fairness and transparency, safeguarding privacy, developing explainable AI, considering societal impact, establishing accountability mechanisms, and engaging in continuous learning, AI developers can effectively fulfill their ethical responsibility. By adhering to these guidelines, developers can contribute to the responsible development

and deployment of AI systems that benefit society while minimizing potential harm.

www.ingramcontent.com/pod-product-compliance
Lightning Source LLC
Chambersburg PA
CBHW062117220526
45471CB00010B/3771